A Southern Star for Maryland

LAWRENCE M. DENTON

A Southern Star for Maryland

Maryland and the Secession Crisis, 1860–1861

PUBLISHING CONCEPTS
BALTIMORE, MARYLAND

Published jointly by Denton & Associates, P.O. Box 468, Queenstown, Maryland, 21658 and Publishing Concepts • Baltimore, Baltimore, Maryland, 21210

Manufactured in the United States of America

First Edition

ISBN: 0-9635159-3-4

Library of Congress catalog card number 95-074770

This work is dedicated to

Dr. Theodore M. Whitfield
Professor of History
Western Maryland College

Born: May 24, 1905   Died: March 21, 1991

Contents

Foreword

Early in this volume Larry Denton quotes the late Maryland U. S. Senator, George L. P. Radcliffe's comment that despite much information on the subject of Maryland and her possible secession in 1861, the information generally was "so partisan and biased in character" and so contradictory that drawing conclusions was "hazardous." Radcliffe as a young graduate student at the Johns Hopkins University wrote his doctoral dissertation on Governor Thomas Holliday Hicks (1857–1861), using a large collection of Hicks's papers which soon thereafter mysteriously disappeared. Scholars therefore have depended heavily on Radcliffe's work for this data.

There have been numerous efforts to prove that Maryland would have seceded if left to her own devices and not "suppressed" by President Lincoln and the national military and naval forces. No writer has been able to write with any certainty what effect Maryland's secession (had it developed) would have had on Maryland or the Confederacy, or on efforts to preserve the Union.

The basic dispute was states' rights versus national rights. Southern states believed as a group the national government had no right to coerce them nor to deprive them of their true share of funds for internal improvements, nor to force higher tariffs on them—among other grievances. They also asserted that the president had no power to suspend the right to a writ of habeas corpus; rather, Congress alone could do so.

President Lincoln defended his actions to preserve the Union, to suppress the insurrection, and to issue a call for troops. He termed secession an unconstitutional act, not allowed by the Constitution of 1787 (written by the delegations of the states and ratified by the people of the states). It was not a Constitution inflicted on the states by the national government. The states had powers reserved to them in the 1787 Constitution, shared some other powers with the national government, and delegated additional clear-cut powers to the national govemment.

Article VI of the U. S. Constitution calls the Constitution the "supreme law of the land" and states that the "judges in every state shall be bound thereby, any thing in the Constitution or laws of any State to the contrary notwithstanding." This supremacy would be in evidence particularly in time of war, economic depression, and other emergencies. In the Civil War either the Union would be preserved or it would be greatly diminished, or destroyed.

Maryland's role in the Civil War was particularly difficult. If she seceded, theoretically the Union might collapse since the capital of the United States would be entrapped in Confederate-held territory. Or the capital might be relocated to Pennsylvania or elsewhere.

Maryland by blood ties, by sentiment, by her general culture, was more akin to the South than to the North. Economically her affiliation was greater with the North, and growing more so. Until Lincoln called for troops, Union sentiment prevailed over secession in Maryland. But even modern polling expertise would be unpredictable on such a question.

Author Larry Denton presents his case after several years of intensive reading, research, study, consultations, and assimilation of his findings. The result of his efforts is a well-written and thoughtful production. He concludes that Maryland would have seceded had not the national government prevented it. This topic has been worked over many times. There is no significant new information. Some of the old materials have been given some new interpretation. These offer opportunities for additional work. A lot of history is being rewritten.

I commend this book to anyone seriously interested in Maryland and the Civil War.

CHARLES BRANCH CLARK

Preface

In the fall of 1963, I was a student of Professor Theodore M. Whitfield, Chairman of the History Department at Western Maryland College, who also served as chairman of the Committee on History, Theme, and Memorials of the Maryland Civil War Centennial Commission. Whitfield often remarked that the war would have been unquestionably changed had Maryland seceded, for the nation's capital would have been surrounded by enemy territory and one can only speculate about the resulting consequences. It was an intriguing question for a decendant of several old Maryland families. As time permitted, I set about trying to answer the question: Would Maryland have seceded if free to do so?

As is typical of much research, I ended up going in a somewhat different direction from that which I had originally intended. It turned out that the case for Maryland's seceding was stronger than I had anticipated. Data from the census and the *Official Records of the War of the Rebellion,* as well as election results can be construed as very supportive. In addition, many historians who have studied the secession movement in great detail seem to lean toward the notion that Maryland would have seceded had it been free to choose.

Some may view this as a partisan work and, indeed, it is primarily focused on making the case supporting the secession of Maryland. I am hopeful the reader will not find it an overly biased work. I have attempted to cite a variety of historians, from the postwar period to the present, and I relied heavily on the views expressed by actual participants and recorded in the *Official Records.* I have striven to present the views of others in context and to relate the actual events of the day in their proper sequence and as they truly happened.

I am deeply indebted to my three principal reviewers: Professor Charles Branch Clark, Colonel William S. Barney (USAF ret.), and Dr. Lawrence R. Greenwood. Professor Clark's insightful comments and his insistence on supportable and documented conclusions were key to this work. He is a scion of the Clark family of Howard County, Maryland, and has taught American history and the Civil War, including Maryland's role in it, at various institutions of higher education for most of his professional life. His doctoral dissertation, *Politics in Maryland during the Civil War,* which helped inspire this work, can be found at the Maryland Historical Society Library in Baltimore. Colonel Barney, former Vice Commander of the Air Weather Service, lectured in military history at West Point, specifically on the effects of weather on the tactics and logistics of the Civil War. His comments on the historical accuracy and general conclusions of this work were invaluable. Also, many of the vignettes cited are his suggestions. Dr. Greenwood, a Virginian, made many valuable comments from the perspective of a Southerner. His analytical skills were especially important in clarifying the data presented throughout the work. He kept me honest.

I am grateful to many friends and Civil War enthusiasts who added their encouragement over the years. Special appreciation is due to the following who, at critical moments, made valuable contributions: Thomas P. Gore, Johanna Hershey, Joseph C. Maguire, Jr., Edward L. McDill, John R. Parker, R. J. Rockefeller, Louis A. Smith, Elizabeth R. Thibodeau and Dave Bishop of Competition Photos. Thanks to Daniel D. Hartzler and Frederick D. Shroyer for permitting me to use pieces from their wonderful collections of Confederate memorabilia. Also, special recognition is due P. Douglas Manger, president of Manger & Associates, and Frank Speck for so ably assisting in the jacket design. Finally, I am deeply indebted to Robert I. Cottom Jr. for his insightful editing and skillful production of this book.

Anyone who has tackled a project of this kind in his or her spare time can understand the impact it can have on one's freedom. I am indebted to my mother, Evelyn, for her encouragement and for understanding the absences from family gatherings. My brothers, Paul Douglas and Wesley Bayne Denton, also added their encouragement and made helpful comments on the text. Finally, and most importantly, I owe an enormous debt of gratitude to my wife, Susan, who bravely endured so many weekends and evenings alone and who protected my quiet time so passionately.

LMD

Introduction

The subject of this work, whether Maryland, if left to her own devices, would have seceded and joined the Southern Confederacy—THE QUESTION—is important to understanding the critical early months of the Civil War. For if Maryland, which bordered the nation's capital on three sides, had seceded, then Washington would have been surrounded by hostile territory. What would the evacuation of Washington have meant to the people of the North? What would it have meant to the governments of Europe, who wanted Southern cotton so badly they were prepared to recognize the Southern Confederacy? Would the North have been able to launch a war effort with their capital in the hands of the enemy? Bruce Catton captured the point succinctly. "Above everything, it [the U.S. government] had to demonstrate to its own people and to the people in Europe that it was capable of sustaining itself. Whatever it did, it did not dare evacuate Washington. It had to hold Washington at all costs, from the beginning of the war right down to the end."[1]

Maryland obviously did not secede. But would the sentiments and wishes of the majority of her people have carried the state out of the Union, if she were permitted to go peacefully? This work examines the events of the period from November 1860 to November 1861 in an attempt to shed some light on this issue. The official results of the presidential election of 1860, comments from various participants in the conflict, data from the U. S. Census of 1860 and the *Official Records,* as well as the views of historians from the era of the Civil War to the current time, are presented to support the argument that Maryland would have withdrawn from the Union.

A critical point in this larger debate is the disagreement regarding the secession issue in the South, before and after Fort Sumter. Prior to the firing on the fort, ordered by the newly established Confederate government, Southerners were truly divided on the issue of secession. In fact, prior to Sumter most Southerners opposed secession. Chapter 1, "Setting the Stage," attempts to clarify that point. No Southern state, with the exception of South Carolina, was anywhere near united on the issue of secession. But after the firing on Fort Sumter, and President Lincoln's response to it—the Proclamation of Insurrection and call for troops to put down the rebellion—Southerners came together as one and supported secession overwhelmingly, albeit some with great misgivings.

What bound together Southerners of the day into a separate nation willing to wage a war for independence? Most who have studied the era agree that Southerners were strongly opposed to the idea of the federal government using military force to coerce a state to remain in the Union; even more were opposed to the aims and principles of the Republican Party, which, of course, Lincoln represented. Lincoln's proclamation and call for troops clearly meant to Southerners coercion by the use of force, and those actions confirmed their suspicion that the Republicans were out to destroy the South. Without question, the proclamation did galvanize public opinion in the South against the Lincoln administration, and against the North as well. Some argue that this was especially true in the upper South where so much effort had been made by leading citizens to find a peaceful solution to the impending crisis. Many felt that Lincoln simply abandoned those seeking compromise and betrayed the Unionists of the upper South.

Maryland, as the point state of the upper South, was unquestionably tied to the region, and clearly tied to Virginia. Chapter 2, "The Election," presents the results of the presidential election of 1860 for the nation and for Maryland in an effort to demonstrate that the country divided into North *vs.* South. It was truly a sectional election. Very few Southerners voted for either of the two Northern parties; equally, very few Northerners voted for either of the two Southern parties. Maryland, in this election, clearly aligned herself with the South.

Chapter 3, "The State," deals with the crucial role Virginia played in the secession movement in Maryland. Virginia's Unionists led, or were a key part of, the various efforts to find a compromise to the political crisis of early 1861. They controlled the Virginia State Convention, and they opposed secession prior to April 15. Maryland's secessionists were closely tied to the Virginians. Unquestionably, they had a profound impact on the secession movement in Maryland.

What happened after April 15 in Maryland is discussed in chapters 4 and 5. Chapter 4, "The Month," gives the reader a day-by-day account of the critical events that occurred in the state during the month, as they would have been most likely viewed by Maryland's secessionists. Lincoln, with the strong support of his cabinet, and even stronger support from the Northern press, moved rapidly to occupy Maryland with federal military forces. The military not only put Maryland's secessionists on the defensive but effectively cut off Maryland from the South. Chapter 5, "The End," highlights the major events that took place over the summer and fall of 1861 in Maryland: the military occupation of the state, suspension of the writ of habeas corpus, arbitrary arrests of political leaders and other key citizens, suppression of the press, and manipulation of the state election. These events ended the secession movement in Maryland and secured the state, once and for all, to the Union.

Chapter 6, "The Military Issue—More Than Just Numbers," considers the intriguing question of allegiances as measured by which side Marylanders chose to fight for. Finally, Chapter 7, "A Matter of Economics," is a short essay regarding the critical issue of the leanings of the all-important commercial or business class of the state, and how it reacted to the military occupation of its homeland.

Bruce Catton's cogent conclusion regarding Maryland and

THE QUESTION is this: "The state of Maryland was kept in the Union, largely because the people who wanted to take it out of the Union were thrown into jail."[2] This work buttresses that conclusion and elaborates on Marylanders' true feelings regarding secession and joining with the South.

"We hold the fate of your State in our hands."
— *New York Times,* April 21, 1861

1

Setting the Stage

A country with no regard for its past will do little worth remembering in the future.
Abraham Lincoln

In the spring of 1861 the eyes of the nation turned anxiously toward Maryland. A small state, in normal times some would say politically insignificant, it had a relatively small population and modest wealth. But on its southern border lay Washington, D.C., and on April 17, across the Potomac, the Virginia State Convention voted to secede from the Union. Many expected Maryland to follow, leaving the nation's capital surrounded by what might well be considered foreign territory. Had Maryland seceded, subsequent events that fateful spring would have unfolded quite differently from the way they did, perhaps even precluding the great and tragic war that followed.

For the most part, historians agree that Maryland could not have seceded, and obviously she did not. In 1861 many citizens felt that individual states had a right to leave the Union or secede if a majority of a state's citizens voted to do so. The subject of this work is whether Maryland, if left to her own, would have seceded and joined the Southern Confederacy.

A brief look at the decades preceding 1860 is helpful in establishing a context for this discussion. The republic underwent swift and unsettling changes during this period. Population increased rapidly through natural growth and, more troubling to some, immigration. Railroads emerged as a revolutionary new form of transportation, affecting the economy and with it people's lives. Most importantly, the young republic increased its territory exponentially, creating new centers of economic and political power and inflaming sectional tensions.

The political changes were especially disturbing. In the face of new issues the old Whig Party collapsed in the 1850s. The Know-Nothings arose in opposition to ideas and people foreign, then fell, and a new party, the Republicans, organized to challenge the old order. These changes contributed to a growing sense of unease, particularly as the older states of the Union began to cede political power to the newer states of the Northwest and West. This last development was especially alarming for the older states of the South.[1]

Authors for well over a hundred years have offered their analyses of these developments with respect to the secession movement, some from a Southern perspective, some from a Northern one, and some with still a different emphasis of one kind or another. "The data available for a study of the period are numerous; but they are generally so partisan and biased in character, and withal so contradictory, that attempts at drawing conclusions from them are, on the whole, hazardous." So wrote George Radcliffe in the preface of his work, *Governor Thomas H. Hicks of Maryland and the Civil War*. Radcliffe, one of a very few who actually saw Hicks's wartime papers before they were lost, concluded: "The course of events during this period may be traced with a fair amount of assurance, but the influences and the causes which are behind these are wrapt in much obscurity."[2]

The South of 1860–1861 was hardly homogenous. The vast region that stretched from Maryland to western Texas was anything but a physical entity; geographic and economic differences caused a variety of opinions on the important issues of the day. Some of its states faced the Atlantic, some the Gulf of Mexico; some were securely landlocked in the interior, their character drawn by their rivers. "Coastal plains were often sharply divided from the rolling uplands behind them by falls and rapids which marked the end of navigation for ocean-going craft. Farther inland a great chain of mountains rolled south and west from Pennsylvania to Alabama, effectively dividing peoples and interests."[3] The socio-political differences of the section were equally great.

> The South was never more than a bundle of contrasting and conflicting interests, classes, and values. Virginians who lived along the coast below the fall line and South Carolinians who lived in and around Charleston differed sharply in their social-economic status from each other and even more from those who dwelt in the back country of either state. Political conflicts, first in the colonial era and then in national period, disturbed their relationships, shifted their capitals and changed their constitutions. The plainer folk who settled in North Carolina and Georgia never quite matched their neighbors in quality and were never, for long, permitted to forget that fact. The peoples of the Lower South and of Tennessee and Kentucky were Westerners.[4]

The South of 1860-61 was, indeed, quite diverse, and so it is difficult to say just what in the Southern background contributed to the development of distinct sectional qualities. This socio-political diversity naturally found its way into the secession issue. Those in the tidewater thought differently from those in the high country, and recent immigrants differently from established folk. The state votes for or against secession are presented here.

December 20, 1860. South Carolina votes for secession 169–0.

"... the only state in which there was not, in 1861, considerable opposition to withdrawal from the Union was South Carolina."[5]

January 9, 1861. Mississippi votes for secession 84–15.

"In Mississippi there was a respectable minority of cooperationists and Unionists, most of whom were old-time Whigs who opposed secession. Of the ninety-nine delegates elected to the secession convention, about one-fourth were cooperationists and Unionists."[6]

January 10, 1861. Florida votes for secession 62–7.

January 11, 1861. Alabama votes for secession 61–39.

"In Alabama a vigorous minority, drawing from the northern counties, opposed immediate secession."[7]

"In north Alabama . . . the majority of the people opposed leaving the Union in 1861. . . . Thirty-one of the votes cast against the ordinance of secession were cast by delegates from that section.[8]

January 19, 1861. Georgia votes for secession 164–133.

"The situation in Georgia revealed a sharper difference of opinion among prominent leaders and a more vigorous opposition to secession. . . . There was able leadership on both sides [of the movements for or against secession]. . . . Of those opposed to secession . . . the most prominent were Alexander H. Stephens. [later Vice President of the Confederate States of America]."[9]

"Although most of the people in Georgia believed in the right of secession, many of them did not wish to leave the Union in 1861 . . . more than one-third of the delegates voted against secession."[10]

January 26, 1861. Louisiana votes for secession 113–17.

"Though this ordinance was passed by a vote of 113–17, yet

the popular vote for delegates to the convention showed a much smaller proportion of secessionists, the vote being 20,448 for secession as compared to 17,296 against it."[11]

February 1, 1861. Texas votes for secession 166–8.

"The distinguished governor, Sam Houston, was unwavering in his determination to adhere to the Union; but his vigorous efforts against secession were unavailing."[12]

"In Texas . . . there was an element made up largely of old-time Whigs and Germans who bitterly opposed secession and never became reconciled to the Confederacy. . . . The Unionists declared the elections were unfair and insisted that the majority of the people were against secession, an estimate which is hardly probable, although, as later developments show, the opponents of secession were many."[13]

April 17, 1861. Virginia votes for secession 88–55.

"When commissioners from several of the seceded states of the lower south visited Richmond to induce Virginia to secede, the convention resisted their impassioned appeals. . . . On April 4 a motion to draw up an ordinance of secession was voted down, 88 to 45."[14]

"In Virginia practically all of the people in the western part of the state were either ardent Unionists or were apathetic. . . . Although the southwestern section of the state, in which not more than one-fourth of the people favored secession, did not separate from Virginia, it evinced . . . a source of opposition to the attempted enforcement of laws by the Confederate government. . . . [G]eographic and economic conditions made the people west of the mountains more in sympathy with the north than with the south."[15]

May 6, 1861. Arkansas votes for secession 65–5.

"When the members of the convention were elected the popular majority against secession (tested by the vote for delegates to their previous stand) was 5,699 in a total of 43,228. . . . [A]s in Virginia, it was Lincoln's April policy that produced secession. During the days from Lincoln's inauguration to the firing at Sumter the Unionists held sufficient control . . . to prevent the passage of a secession ordinance."[16]

"Northwest Arkansas, in which there was much disloyalty during the war, was almost solidly against secession. . . . The election of Lincoln was not considered a sufficient cause for leaving the Union and men of every party favored all honorable efforts to preserve the Union."[17]

May 7, 1861. Tennessee votes for secession by popular vote 104,913 to 47,238.

"But the people were more Union-minded than the legislature. The proposition to call a convention to consider secession was rejected by popular vote (69,675 to 57,798); while on the issue of secession or no secession the vote (as judged by delegates' commitments) was even more decisive—24,749 for, and 91,803 against . . . The essential fact was that the people of Tennessee . . . were caught in an inescapable dilemma—the dilemma of the Upper South—which gave them no chance to act as they wished (i.e., to proceed with measures for a peaceable restoration of the Union), but forced an immediate choice between two hateful alternatives."[18]

"The eastern part of Tennessee, which after 1861 gave practically no support to the Confederacy and which served as a refuge for the disloyal from all over the South, was almost solid for the Union. . . . The Unionists charged fraud in the election, and East Tennessee attempted to separate from the rest of the state."[19]

May 20, 1861. North Carolina votes for secession 120–0.

"Nowhere was the contrast between the Upper and Lower South better revealed than in the difference between the two Carolinas. It is significant that South Carolina was the first to pass an ordinance of secession, North Carolina was the last. . . . North Carolina did not consider Lincoln's election a sufficient cause for secession. When the legislature, at the prodding of Governor John W. Ellis, submitted to the people a proposition for calling a convention to consider secession, it was defeated, on February 28, by a vote of 47,323 to 46,672."[20]

"Throughout North Carolina there were many zealous Unionists, and until Lincoln called for troops the large majority of the people opposed secession."[21]

In most of the states to join the Southern Confederacy there was ample Unionist sentiment and, indeed, in the Upper South, Union sentiment was stronger than secessionism until Lincoln issued his Proclamation of Insurrection and called for troops to put down the rebellion.

> A brief survey of the secession movement at the beginning of the war reveals the fact that there was considerable opposition to secession in most of the southern states in 1861. . . . In general, those that opposed leaving the Union in 1861 were old-line Whigs, who were either outspoken unionists or unionists at heart, the up-country element, the foreign element, and many others who hoped for an ultimate peaceful settlement of the questions causing trouble.[22]

James G. Randall and David Donald observed, "Whatever the differences of viewpoint in the Upper South, there would seem to have been a prevailing pattern of unionist sentiment against a background of Southernism."[23]

This "pattern of unionist sentiment" is important to the discussion of Maryland and secession because Maryland was a part of the Upper South, and her people acted similarly to reluctant Virginians, North Carolinians, and Tennesseans. Maryland had deep historical and cultural ties to the South, especially to Virginia. "Politically as well as economically, Marylanders traditionally looked south. Sharing a common heritage, forged by the 'peculiar institution' of slavery, Marylanders had strong sympathies for the South."[24]

A compelling piece of evidence to illustrate how divided was the Southern mind on secession is the number of Southerners, both officers and enlisted men, who fought for the Union. Charles Anderson, in *Fighting by Southern Federals* (1912) found that 160 Southerners commanded federal brigades and fought with distinction, and about one-fourth of federal generals were born in the South. Southern-born officers also held numerous colonelcies and other ranks. Anderson surmises that as many as 200,000 Southern-born soldiers fought in Union blue, about half the number that comprised the entire Confederate army in the field at any one time.[25]

These numbers illustrate the lack of unanimity in the South, and among Southerners wherever they lived, on the issue of disunion as measured by the ultimate test—on which side they fought. In the secession winter of 1860-1861, every Southern state with the exception of South Carolina demonstrated significant difference of opinion on the secession issue. It is simply impossible to categorize Southerners of the era—many were avid secessionists, many were staunch Unionists, and many kept to the middle-of-the-road, hoping for some sort of compromise.

However, most historians do agree that on two issues most Southerners were united: a thorough distrust, if not downright hatred of the Republicans; and, a view that the federal government must not use force to coerce any state to stay in the Union. When the Confederate government ordered the firing on Fort Sumter, and when Lincoln responded by issuing his April 15 Proclamation of Insurrection and call for troops, it simply united

Southerners and Northerners alike. Everyone was forced to take sides, and most Southerners would choose to stay with their section. Lincoln's call for troops to put down the rebellion meant the use of military force. A detailed discussion of this coming together of Southerners and its impact on the secession movement in Maryland is presented in chapter 4.

Another background issue, as previously mentioned, was the changing landscape of national and Maryland politics during the 1840s and 1850s. Although this was a time of great political change in the nation, for most of the first half of the nineteenth century politics in Maryland could best be described as relatively stable. The Whigs and the Democrats were the two dominant parties, party loyalty was high, and electioneering was fun. Elections were spirited, of high interest to the electorate, and usually very close. Most citizens voted enthusiastically.

> Intense and competitive, politics in the 1840s was also a highly sociable and pleasurable activity. In an age of few formal recreations, Marylanders enjoyed the steamboat rides, barbecues, and dances organized by political parties. . . . Fall picnics were perhaps the most popular political activity. In 1844 thirty thousand Baltimoreans crowded into Gibson's woods to enjoy a Defender's Day picnic where Democratic appeals and speeches flowed as freely as the party's hard cider.[26]

However, by the 1850s the political landscape was changing dramatically. Agitation from Baltimore and the western counties for more representation in the General Assembly finally became so great that a convention was called to write a new state constitution. The Constitution of 1851 gave the northwestern counties and Baltimore City more representation in the legislature, created more elective offices, and weakened the power of the governor. Following this came the presidential election of 1852, which witnessed a peculiar lethargy in the state and resulted in the Democrats carrying Maryland for Franklin Pierce. But the loss by the Whig candidate, General Winfield Scott, was much more than just another election loss—it signalled the beginning of what turned out to be a rapid collapse of the entire Whig Party, both locally and nationally. The significance of this was that the Whigs—the party of the landed gentry, of the old conservatives, the party of stability—ceased to exist in a matter of a few years.

> By 1855, Maryland Whigs found themselves members of what one called "the rump of a broken down and discredited faction." To Democrats, these 35,000 ex-Whigs represented an attractive and uncommitted constituency to be courted throughout the decade; for other Marylanders the politics of the 1850s meant a confusing period of political transition marked by new parties, issues, and leaders.[27]

Into this political void came the Know-Nothing or American Party—one of those strange anomalies that infrequently strike American politics. At this time of enormous change—economic, social, and political—the Know-Nothings answered with nativism and anti-Catholic (viz. anti-immigrant) sentiment. Theirs was a general opposition to change, which they blamed on immigrants and to some extent on the Catholics (who represented the control of a foreign Pope, etc.). They rose to power rapidly and departed just as quickly. From 1855 to 1859 they controlled the state with their primary strength in Baltimore City and former Whig strongholds. They were best known for their secrecy, their intimidation of opponents and, in Baltimore, for their illegal and brutal actions on election days.

In fact Maryland elections became truly dangerous affairs in the 1850s, particularly in the city of Baltimore, where gang violence had long before given the city the name of "mobtown." City fire companies had long fought one another for the privilege of putting out fires (and collecting insurance money) and before long political clubs, often manned by the young and underemployed in a tempestuous city, had joined the fray. With names like the Plug Uglies (over a thousand strong), Rip Raps, and Blood Tubs, the clubs took political sides and also took up arms, including cannon. In the municipal elections of 1855, the better element called upon Mayor Hinks (a Know-Nothing) to order the city militia under General George Steuart (later a general in the Confederate army) to hold themselves in readiness to protect the polls.

On October 8, election day, the disorders at the polls exceeded anything known before. What amounted to an infantry engagement took place in Lexington Market. The Know-Nothings captured a Democratic stronghold and triumphantly sacked it. Know-Nothing Thomas Swann was declared elected by a majority of 1,575. The scene was well set for the drama that followed in the presidential election of 1856.[28]

Another election practice abetted the influence of the gangs. Ballots were printed, often with distinctive markings, and voters had to carry them to the ballot box, in full view of critical gang members and partisan election judges. Failure to increase the number of voting places in Baltimore forced as many as four thousand citizens to vote at one window. Carrying a striped or colored ballot, a voter had to make his way through a potentially hostile crowd to an election judge who could be far from friendly. It was here that gangs practiced intimidation to the fullest—taunts and jeers frequently turned to aggravated assault.

By 1859 the good citizens had begun to assert themselves and gain control of this outrageous situation. In the municipal election of October 1859, the Reform Association was partially successful. . . . The General Assembly of 1860 met on January 4, and enacted into law the recommendations of the Reform Committee of Baltimore. . . . the Legislature declared null and

void the election of the 2d of November. . . . On the 10th of
October Mayor Brown and a Reform council were elected by a
majority of nearly two to one. This election marked the end of
the domination of the Know-Nothing Party in the city of Baltimore and the State of Maryland, although the party still held
over in the executive department, as Governor Hicks's term of
office had two more years to run.[29]

By the fall of 1859 and early in 1860, having attained and lost
control of the legislature, the Know-Nothing Party began to fade.
At this critical moment, many Marylanders were left without a
political party—a void into which the Democratic Party
promptly stepped, aided by unsettling events. The most notable,
for Maryland and the South, was John Brown's raid on Harper's
Ferry in October 1859. It electrified the nation, especially Maryland and Virginia, within whose borders Brown had brought the
violence of Kansas, where he had gained his terrible reputation.
The raid sent shock waves through every slaveholding state.
Nothing, it seemed, so captivated the whites of the day as the
prospect of a slave insurrection. Maryland's Democrats (with
impeccable timing), having just captured control of the General
Assembly, seized the initiative and moved quickly to demonstrate to the electorate that they would take charge of the
situation. Brown's raid, and the sympathy with which many in
the Northern states regarded him, intensified Southern bitterness. In that climate Maryland's legislature, resolved to quell any
outbreaks among blacks and prevent abolitionists from fostering
such uprisings, appropriated $70,000 for arms and military
equipment to be distributed to military companies throughout
the state.[30]

This put arms in the hands of local militia groups, which, for the most part were controlled by Democrats. It also began the process (mental and military) of preparing the state to defend itself in a time of high anxiety and true consternation for many old-line Maryland families. Also at this time, Marylanders, like most Southerners, found a scapegoat in the Republicans, the party of the hated abolitionists, the party which seemed to continually attack the South, and the party which fostered drastic change in the way things were. This distrust and hatred of the Republican Party is important to an understanding of Marylanders' feelings about secession, because when forced to choose a side, most Marylanders would choose against the Republicans.

The point of this work is to explore how the secessionists fared in Maryland during this period of great change and uneasiness, when the South was truly divided on the secession issue. For the divided South substantially affected the issue of secession in Maryland. It was the strength of the unionist movement in the upper South that kept Maryland from moving toward secession in early 1861. Maryland was linked to the upper South, especially Virginia, and simply could not act on secession until the states between her and the seceded states of the lower South acted. On April 15, 1861, Lincoln's Proclamation of Insurrection and call for troops to put down the rebellion begun three days earlier at Fort Sumter, forced all to choose sides. It electrified the nation, uniting the sections against one another. The Northern response to Lincoln's call for troops was so strong and came so quickly that Maryland was overrun by Northern troops before she could take action to unite with the South. But first to the election of 1860, which so clearly demonstrated that the nation had divided along sectional lines.

2

The Election

*"Secession is nothing but revolution. . . . Still a Union that can only
be maintained by swords and bayonets, . . . has no charm for me."*
                                                          Robert E. Lee

The presidential election of 1860, the most bitterly sectional
political contest in American history, struck the border states
particularly hard. With their economic and social ties to both
regions, the voters in the border states had to weigh political ideals
and long-time allegiances against self-interest. An examination of
the election results in Maryland, as measured against the background of national patterns, will suggest how Maryland compared
to the states in the upper South that joined the Confederacy. It will
also show who voted for whom in the state and whether there was
a connection between support for a given candidate with a level
of support for either the North or the South.

Occasionally in the first eighty-odd years of the Republic a
presidential election had been held with three serious candidates. This usually resulted in some abnormality, and once the
House of Representatives even had to choose the president. But
in 1860, as established political parties shattered and attempted
to reform, there appeared four serious candidates backed by four
serious parties to divide the electorate in different ways. Faced
with four choices, the electorate divided between two extremist

parties, one in the North and one in the South; and, two moderate parties, again one in each section. "From a national perspective," wrote one observer, ". . . the party system and the country itself were headed toward spectacular trouble in 1860."[1]

Before examining the election of 1860 and what the results meant relative to the question of Maryland's course in the crisis, we must first look at the four parties—their candidates, their platforms and their appeal. As mentioned, the electorate was faced with two extremist parties and two moderate parties. The extremist parties were those with strong, uncompromising positions, whereas the moderate parties favored some form of compromise on the major issues if it meant saving the Union. First, an examination of the two extremist parties, the Southern Democrats and the Republicans.

The Southern Democratic Party came into existence in April 1860 as a result of the breakup of the old Democratic Party at its convention in Charleston, South Carolina. The Democratic Party, which for years under the leadership of Stephen Douglas and others had managed to find compromises on the great sectional issues, came apart in the spring of 1860. From the outset at Charleston, delegates from different sections of the country faced one another with bitterness and mistrust. Some of the more radical Southern Democrats wanted reassurance that the party would side with them more strongly. They charged that Northern Democrats with abetting abolitionist agitation by refusing to "take a determined stand in defense of Southern rights." Those rights included the protection of slavery in the expanding western territories—the most explosive issue of the time. Southerners demanded the party adopt a resolution calling on the federal government to protect slave property "wherever it should be taken." But Democrats from the Northern states could not openly embrace slavery. "This was a statement which they could not make, nor could they recognize the principle by indirection. Such a concession would have resulted in the defection of thousands of voters in their own section and insured, beyond possibility of retrieval, the defeat of the party in the election."[2]

So the old Democratic Party split, unable to resolve this troubling issue. The Southern wing, at a convention in Baltimore in June, nominated former Vice President John C. Breckinridge of Kentucky for president, and Joseph Lane of Oregon for vice president. The candidates were regarded as moderates, that is, they were not of the fire-eaters, and were chosen, at least partially, for their potential appeal to voters of more moderate views. Their platform, however, was anything but moderate—it stood for the protection of slavery at all costs, advocated the rights of states over those of the federal government, and generally lauded the rights of the South and repudiated the principles of "Black Republicans." "These self-described National Democrats endorsed the Dred Scott decision, protested northern agitation against 'the institutions of slave states,' and insisted that the provisions of the Fugitive Slave Act be upheld."[3]

They were state-rights men to the last and no one misunderstood that. They considered the federal government an agent of the sovereign states, entrusted with certain carefully defined powers for the performance of specific duties. They regarded the Constitution as an instrument of union between states that had never surrendered nor agreed to unlimited submission to the government created by the compact. The states, they maintained, and not the government so created, were the final judges of the extent of their reserved powers.[4] The Breckinridge Democrats, as they became known, were strongly proslavery, adamantly for states rights and for the South—and even though they denied it during formal electioneering, they left no doubt that they would have no part in a country led by a "Black Republican," Abraham Lincoln. In the event of his election, they would promote secession. Yet by forming their own party, the Southern Democrats did exactly what they had for so long accused the Republicans of doing—they created a purely sectional party.

But in the South of 1860 there was substantial resistance to the Southern Democrats and their most vociferous fire-eating leaders, William Lowndes Yancey of Alabama and South Carolinian Robert Barnwell Rhett. The *Southern Advocate*, an Alabama newspaper among many,

> ... objected bitterly to the Yancey group "prating of Southern Rights as if they were the whole South," talking "of Southern interests as if they owned all the negroes in the South," shouting about "Southern honor as if they were the only people in the South!" It would have the nation know that there were "planters, farmers, working and business men" in the South who could "not be dictated to nor led by the nose." They could think for themselves, and they did not think as did Yancey.[5]

For the voter, then, the Southern Democratic Party represented an uncompromising stance on slavery, the primacy of states rights, and above all, a repudiation of abolitionism.

The other party of uncompromising positions in 1860 was the Republican Party. Starting from a base of support in New England and the Old Northwest in the 1850s, the party had steadily grown in strength and found support along the Atlantic seaboard, the Midwest, and the Northwest. By 1858 they had a plurality in the House of Representatives and were clearly a force to be reckoned with on the national scene. But it was hardly monolithic. Like all American political parties the Republicans were "rather a mass of diverse elements loosely cemented together by a common purpose to stop the spread of slavery. There were former Democrats and former Whigs; former Know-Nothings and immigrants from Germany; old free-soilers and ultra abolitionists. There was, too, a sectional difference between the Northwest, which wanted to prohibit the further extension of slavery, and the Northeast, which opposed the institution wherever it existed."[6]

In May 1860, Republicans gathered in Chicago, and although the party was stocked with well-known political leaders, they had great difficulty in selecting a nominee. They passed over such notables as William H. Seward, Edward Bates, Salmon P. Chase, Nathaniel P. Banks, and Simon Cameron to settle finally on the relatively unknown and untried Abraham Lincoln, a compromise candidate of the convention regarded as a moderate. Born in the South, and a former Whig, Lincoln was hoped to possess national appeal. However, just as in the case with Breckinridge, it was the party platform that proved more extreme than the candidate. The platform "denied that slavery was based in the common law, denied the right of Congress or of a territorial legislature to establish it in any of the territories, denounced the principle of non-intervention and popular sovereignty as deceptions and frauds, and defined the doctrine of the right of secession as treason." Though some at the North saw the platform and the selection of a moderate candidate as the party's repudiation of its radical anti-slavery wing, that was not how the results of the Chicago Convention were received at the South. When Republicans began circulating abolitionist senator Charles Sumner's antislavery tract, *Barbarism of Slavery,* and Hinton Rowan Helper's *Impending Crisis* as campaign documents, they demonstrated what Southerners perceived to be their true colors. Southerners denounced the Chicago platform as "a rebuke to Southern morality, and a gross insult to Southern intelligence."[7]

For the Southerner, Republicans were to be hated because they were the party of the despised abolitionists—those people who had attacked the South and stirred up the Negroes for over a decade. The bloodshed in Kansas, fomented, Southerners thought, by the likes of the New England Emigrant Aid Society, which sent arms to free state settlers, came eastward in the fall of 1859 in the person of John Brown of "Osawatomie." Brown's raid on the United States arsenal at Harper's Ferry, Virginia, on October 16, and subsequent reports all through the next year of abolition-inspired slave uprisings and murderous riots of free blacks, of towns burned down in Texas and women and children murdered, produced a "state of near hysteria" in much of the South throughout the election season.[8] Thus, despite political maneuvering, despite carefully worded platforms, Southerners perceived Republicans as extremists. For the Southern voter whatever his party choice, the Republican message must have been unmistakably clear—they were antislavery, against states rights, and against the South.

Still, much of the nation, probably an overwhelming majority, would have defined itself as moderate in 1860, and in this crisis two parties of moderation arose—the regular Democratic Party or the Douglas Democrats as they became known, and the newly formed Constitutional Union Party.

After the break-up of the April convention in Charleston, Democrats reconvened in Baltimore in June 1860—that is, most of the Democrats. Some of the Southern delegates refused to attend and assembled instead in Richmond. But in Baltimore, the Democrats had no more luck than they had had in Charleston, for the party was hopelessly divided between its Northern and Southern wings. They split again, this time for good. The regular Democrats nominated Stephen A. Douglas for the presidency and a moderate Georgian, Herschel V. Johnson, for the vice-presidency. The Democratic platform was essentially that of 1856—opposition to congressional interference with slavery, support of the decisions by the Supreme Court on the slavery issue, enforcement of the Fugitive Slave Law, and, of course, support of Douglas's doctrine of popular sovereignty, which was intended to let the inhabitants of the territories decide the slavery question but which had led, in fact, to open warfare in Kansas. They meant to be the party of moderation. Having won the election of 1856 on this platform, they felt they were the only remaining truly national party. They stood for cooperation and compromise, and above all else for preserving the old union.

During the campaign they appealed to these sentiments and aggressively attacked Breckinridge Democrats as harshly as they struck at Republicans. The Yancey-Rhett "fire-eaters," they maintained, had deliberately broken up the party at Charleston by insisting on a platform that aggressively protected slavery, and they had produced a Southern Democratic ticket repulsive to Northern moderates, one that would split the party and surely elect Lincoln and result in secession.[9] "If you desire dissolution of the Union, vote for Breckinridge; if you desire the disruption of democracy, vote for Breckinridge,"[10] the Frederick, *Maryland Union* stated on November 1, 1860. The Douglas Democrats would let the courts decide on slavery, reject the extremists of both sides, work for compromise as in the past, and preserve the Union. The party represented the moderate voter in the North.

Perhaps the most interesting phenomenon of the presidential election of 1860 was the coming together of a wide range of moderates to form the Constitutional Union Party. This party began to organize in the spring of 1860—although various political leaders had been promoting an opposition party for more than a year—out of the fear of extremism and the desire of a large number of citizens to hold the Union together. "The Union as It Was," became their campaign slogan. The party had its origins in the borderland, particularly in the slaveholding states of the upper South, but enjoyed widespread support throughout the South.

In the years since the Revolution, the border states had grown away from the deep South. Border state agriculture began to resemble Northern agriculture, not the Cotton Kingdom, and cities like Baltimore, Richmond, Louisville, Nashville, and Memphis had begun to develop industries and become commercial centers with necessary ties to Northern markets. Slavery had changed its character in these states as well. Maryland had the largest free black population of any state, and the institution in the upper south was generally weakening. Then, too, the party's "the Union as it was" slogan aptly reflected the "fundamentally conservative, Union-loving attitude of the majority of the Southern people. Douglas owed his Southern support to the existence of such an attitude, but there were many who distrusted him and were ready for a new party based on the old Whig principle of national harmony."[11]

The Constitutional Unionists convened in Baltimore in May 1860. From the outset they were determined to avoid controversy and promote harmony. To do this they adopted a platform that called for preserving the Union, preserving the Constitution, and enforcing the laws of the land. They avoided the slavery question and emphasized national patriotism. A newspaper correspondent observed that the delegates believed the country was "weary of the whole theme of slavery and irrepressible conflict, and would rally to the standard of a party which rigorously avoided any mention of them."[12] The convention was attended by many well-known senior statesmen from both sections, but it was dominated by men from the slave holding Border States. They nominated for president John Bell, the head of the old Whig Party in Tennessee, and Edward Everett of Massachusetts for vice president. Everett would later be the principal speaker in the dedication ceremony at Gettysburg, where Lincoln delivered his memorable address. Both men had had long and distinguished careers in public life. On the surface they were probably the two best qualified candidates in the election.

Their platform favored states' rights and thus appealed to many Southern voters. It was, wrote one historian, "a distinctly Southern platform. It did not pledge its endorsers to support the union of states at all hazards. It pledged them to reestablish the rights of the people and of the states, and to restore the principles of justice and fraternity and equality as fundamental principles in government action, because those were the terms and the conditions of the Constitution."[13]

The Constitutional Union Party represented leadership by senior statesmen whose aims would be stability, compromise, and preservation of the Union, "as it was." And "as it was" meant a Union where states' rights and protection of Southern interests were guaranteed.

The Constitutional Unionists represented the moderate voter in the South. Because an understanding of this point—that they represented the vote of the moderate South—is so central to the conclusion of this chapter, a further analysis of the Constitutional Unionists is contained in a postscript to this chapter.

The Marylander of 1860 was confronted therefore with the following choices:

VOTE SOUTHERN DEMOCRAT—a vote for the preservation of slavery, for states' rights, for the South, and against Northern interference—the uncompromising Southern vote;

VOTE REPUBLICAN—a vote for abolition of slavery, against states' rights, and against the South—the extremist Northern vote;

VOTE DOUGLAS DEMOCRAT—a vote to reject the radicals of both North and South, a vote to compromise on the issues and to preserve the Union—the moderate Northern vote;

VOTE CONSTITUTIONAL UNION—a vote to reject the radicals of both North and South, a vote to compromise on the issues, to preserve the Union, and—again this is the critical difference from the Douglas Democrats—a vote for states' rights and the protection of Southern interests. This was the moderate Southern vote.

Later in this chapter, these choices for the Marylander will be examined at the state level, county by county. But first a review of the results of the presidential election of 1860 from the national perspective. Historians have analyzed the election of 1860 extensively. Table 1 presents the popular vote in 1860 and demonstrates the degree of sectionalism in the election by showing where the candidates drew their support.[14] The division between sections is clear, and note the similarity of Maryland's vote to that of the states of the upper South who later joined the Confederacy.

The total for Lincoln is informative. He received 98.6 percent of his vote from the North and only 1.4 percent from the South. The total for Breckinridge was somewhat skewed because of the unusually large vote he received in Pennsylvania, but, if we discount that, nearly 87 percent of his vote came from the South. These were the two extremist candidates, and although there were some exceptions, by and large the voter of 1860 who cast his vote for either of these two candidates probably did so with a clear view of what his vote stood for—a vote for slavery, states' rights, and the South; or a vote against slavery and states' rights.

The vote for these uncompromising positions is important, because the extremists, and they had relatively large numbers, forced the moderates to take sides and drove the nation apart. The election of 1860 drew the lines deeply: the extremists out-voted the moderates, 58 percent to 42 percent, a figure derived by comparing the total vote of Lincoln and Breckinridge

TABLE 1

Popular Vote in the Election of 1860

NORTH

State	Lincoln	Douglas	Breckinridge	Bell
California	39,173	38,516	34,334	6,817
Connecticut	43,792	15,522	14,641	3,291
Illinois	172,161	160,215	2,404	4,913
Indiana	139,033	115,509	12,295	5,306
Iowa	70,409	55,111	1,048	1,763
Maine	62,811	26,693	6,368	2,046
Massachusetts	106,533	34,372	5,939	22,331
Michigan	88,480	65,057	805	405
Minnesota	22,069	11,920	748	62
New Hampshire	37,519	25,881	2,112	441
New Jersey	58,324	62,810	—	—
New York	362,646	312,510	—	—
Ohio	231,610	187,232	11,405	12,194
Oregon	5,270	3,951	5,006	183
Pennsylvania	268,030	16,765	178,871	12,776
Rhode Island	12,224	7,707	—	—
Vermont	33,808	8,649	1,866	217
Wisconsin	86,110	65,021	888	161
Total Northern Vote	1,840,022	1,213,432	278,730	72,906
% of candidate's vote from North	98.6	88.1	13*	12.4

SOUTH

State	Lincoln	Douglas	Breckinridge	Bell
Alabama	—	13,651	48,831	27,875
Arkansas	—	5,227	28,732	20,094
Delaware	3,815	1,023	7,337	3,864
Florida	—	367	8,543	5,437
Georgia	—	11,590	51,889	42,886
Kentucky	1,364	25,651	53,143	66,058
Louisiana	—	7,625	22,861	20,204
Maryland	2,294	5,966	42,482	41,760
Mississippi	—	3,283	40,797	25,040
Missouri	17,028	58,801	31,317	58,372
North Carolina	—	2,701	48,539	44,990
South Carolina	—	—	—	—
Tennessee	—	11,350	64,709	69,274
Texas	—	—	47,548	15,438
Virginia	1,929	16,290	74,323	74,681
Total Southern Vote	26,430	163,525	571,051	515973
% of candidate's vote from South	1.4	11.9	87*	87.6
Total popular vote	1,866,452	1,376,957	849,781	588,879

*Excludes the vote from Pennsylvania

to the total vote of Douglas and Bell. As previously noted, the Republicans and the Southern Democrats were diametrically opposed—they were for or against slavery, for or against states' rights, and for preserving the Union only if it was a Union of their definition. J. Thomas Scharf, Maryland's postwar historian, noted that when Lincoln and the Republican or antislavery party attained power, the South was "filled . . . with dismay."

> The South had watched with anxiety the growth of the antislavery party for years. Its people had heard and remembered the taunts, the abuse and the threats which for a long time had been poured fourth against them and their institutions, by the press, the pulpit, and the politicians of the North. They had seen their friends murdered or imprisoned for seeking to maintain their rights. They had seen the officers of the Federal government meet with forcible resistance while endeavoring to enforce the process of the courts in behalf of Southern citizens. They had seen the legislatures of various States enact laws for the purpose of nullifying an Act of Congress, passed to protect the South. It is equally impossible, we think, for any unprejudiced man to study it, and still deny that the Southern States had grave cause to distrust and dread the North.[15]

What had happened to that great body of moderates, the majority of the electorate, who in the early years of the Republic had maintained the center course? Like the more extreme elements, moderates, too, split along sectional lines. The Douglas Democrats represented the moderates of the North, whence Douglas received 88.1 percent of his vote, easily the vast majority of moderate votes in virtually every Northern state. Constitutional Unionists, representing Southern moderates, furnished Bell with 87.6 percent of his total. Northerners simply did not support the Constitutional Unionists, and Southerners refused to support the Douglas Democrats.

The moderates of 1860 were often described as old, out of step, or lacking vigor. In describing the Constitutional Unionists' convention, Scharf observed that it "was regarded, 'as a collection of political antiquities.' The invitation of these highly respected but somewhat obsolete politicians upon the stage of action, was responded to by only twenty-two states."[16] They also suffered from a lack of clarity with the electorate, but that, of course, was sound political strategy. By keeping their platform silent on the most pressing issues, they hoped to bypass the crisis by leaving a degree of freedom for state party organizations to tailor platforms suitable to their local constituencies, much like what the Douglas Democrats had hoped to do at Charleston. But whereas the Douglas Democrats had "wanted an ambiguous platform which could be interpreted one way at the South and another at the North," the Constitutional Unionists "wished to leave each section unhampered by the necessity of interpretation."[17] Nevertheless, in the end the moderates could not generate enough appeal to dominate the electorate, and this division along sectional lines further weakened their overall position in the election returns.

One other observation is of interest to this discussion—a brief look at the outcome of the election in the states of the upper South. Kentucky and Missouri gave large portions of their vote to Northern candidates, in fact Douglas, the candidate of the moderate North, made the strongest showing in Missouri and received a large vote in Kentucky. Maryland, on the other hand, gave only 9 percent of her vote to Northern candidates (the combined totals for Lincoln and Douglas), and more closely resembled Virginia, North Carolina, and Tennessee. Two general conclusions regarding Maryland can be made:

(1) As illustrated in Table 1, the extremists in the country were clearly divided along sectional lines. In Maryland, the extremist vote was clearly Southern. Breckinridge received over 42,000

votes, narrowly carrying the state, while Lincoln received only a handful of votes. Those in Maryland who rejected political compromise aligned themselves with the South.

(2) Also illustrated in Table 1, the moderates in the country divided along sectional lines, but again the moderates of Maryland were clearly Southern. Bell received over 41,000 votes and nearly carried the state, while Douglas received fewer than 6,000 votes. Again, Maryland aligned herself with the South, not the border.

The conclusion to be drawn is that, based on the results of the last free election in Maryland before the war, Marylanders lined up solidly with the South, casting 91 percent of their vote for candidates favoring or supportive of that section of the country. The Northern candidates, Lincoln and Douglas, received only token support in Maryland, as they did in every other seceding Southern state. Thus, the data suggest that the leaders of Maryland, if free to choose their own course, would have followed the preferences expressed by Marylanders in the 1860 presidential election by staying with their section and joining the states of the upper South in the Southern Confederacy.

An important postscript to the national election results is that Lincoln won the presidency without the Southern vote. In the days and weeks following the presidential election of 1860, Southerners came to realize that they had truly lost their power in national politics. "By sweeping the North, Lincoln had accomplished the unprecedented feat of winning the presidency without needing southern support. That stunning demonstration of apparent southern political powerlessness in the Union probably fueled the secession movement as much as any other single factor."[18]

Who voted for whom in Maryland, and the South? Did plantation owners, those with large numbers of slaves—the slaveholding oligarchy—push the South, and Maryland, toward support of the extremist candidate, John Breckinridge? This is an important issue, because if large slaveholders did not support the extremists, where did the latter get their strength and what implications does this have for our discussion? In an attempt to understand this complex issue, the work of David Thomas and Daniel Crofts will be reviewed.[19]

"More than one historian has been puzzled by the attitude of the non-slaveholding whites of the South toward slavery," Thomas wrote, noting that only a minority of Southern voters had any real interest in slavery and that the number of large slaveholders was actually quite small—fewer than eight thousand across the South. Many of those classed as slaveholders, he added, were merely laborers who owned one or two slaves and worked alongside them. He went on to note that many of the large slaveholders were former Whigs—the old conservatives—and not at all in step with radical Southern Democrats.[20] Still, they were numerous enough to act collectively and did so by forming the Constitutional Union Party and by casting a sizable number of their votes for Bell.

On the other hand, Thomas found that nonslaveholding whites in the South tended to vote for Breckinridge. He noted that the counties with many large plantations—counties not dominated by nonslaveholding whites—tended to vote for Bell, the moderate candidate. He concluded, "This would seem to indicate a tendency toward conservatism in the wealthy slaveholding counties and toward radicalism in the poorer counties where there were fewer slaveholders." "Here was a great crisis in which the planters were primarily concerned, yet few of them came forward as leaders."[21] Crofts, on the other hand, found no relationship between slaveholding and party allegiance in the upper South. "In Virginia and Tennessee, slaveowning bore scant relationship to party affiliation. . . . And because both North Carolina parties were proslavery 'without reservation,' effective mobilization of voters . . . must have required an emphasis on issues unrelated to slavery."[22]

Many factors contributed to voting patterns—ties to family, influential friends, personal acquaintance with a given candidate or an elector, even whiskey. And, of course, there is the matter of party loyalty. Crofts's work emphasizes that former party allegiances did play an important role in the presidential election of 1860. Southern moderates were brought together by a desire to see the Union preserved. "Southern moderates, composed primarily of former Whigs from the upper South, had a mixture of motives. They were alarmed by the erosion of national parties and feared the Union would be endangered by continued North-South controversy." These Southern moderates, though, could not unite behind a single candidate. "Most southern Whigs rallied instinctively behind John Bell" and the vice presidential nominee, Edward Everett of Massachusetts, "a respected northern Whig," who strengthened Bell's claim to "nationality." Bell's party simply could not embrace the Democrats. "Constitutional Union Party managers hoped to exploit the division of the Democratic Party."

This naturally posed a dilemma for moderate Democrats in the South. Several factors, Crofts argued, combined to keep a separate Douglas ticket on the ballot there. First, the Douglas Democrats were the "political home for many Irish-and German-American voters, who felt they had no place else to go." They were repelled equally by the suspected disunionism of the Breckinridge Democracy and by the nativist taint of the Constitutional Unionists. Then, too, the bitterness of the party split at

TABLE 2

Maryland Popular Vote in the Election of 1860

Subdivision	Lincoln	Douglas	Breckinridge	Bell
Allegany	520	1,202	979	1,521
Anne Arundel	3	98	1,017	1,041
Baltimore	37	449	3,305	3,388
Calvert	1	43	387	399
Caroline	12	100	616	712
Carroll	59	334	1,799	2,294
Cecil	158	393	1,506	1,792
Charles	6	38	723	430
Dorchester	35	31	1,176	1,262
Frederick	103	437	3,176	3,617
Garrett*	—	—	—	—
Harford	81	82	1,528	1,862
Howard	1	189	530	830
Kent	42	74	694	852
Montgomery	50	99	1,125	1,155
Prince George's	1	43	1,048	885
Queen Anne's	0	87	879	908
St. Mary's	1	190	920	261
Somerset	2	96	1,338	1,536
Talbot	2	98	898	793
Washington	95	282	2,479	2,567
Wicomico	—	—	—	—
Worcester	0	212	1,425	1,059
Baltimore City	1,087	1,503	14,957	12,604
Total	2,296	6,080	42,505	41,768
Percentage	2.5	6.5	45.9	45.1

*Not formed

Source: John T. Willis, *Presidential Elections in Maryland* (Mt. Airy, Md.: Lomond Publications, Inc., 1984).

Charleston made reconciliation difficult. "The poisonous division of the Democratic Party in 1860 left Douglas loyalists vengeful toward what they perceived as the secession-minded bolters."

But in the end, few Southerners opted to support Douglas, and he received only token votes in the South. "The election returns revealed that voters in the upper South had clung to traditional party allegiances." It appears that former Whigs lent their support to Bell and the vast majority of Democratic voters supported Breckinridge.[23]

Most historians agree that the Constitutional Union Party was made up primarily of old Southern Whigs, who counted among their members many of the great planters of the day. These cast their vote for Bell, because the wealthy of any society tend to be more conservative, having the most to lose with any radical change and preferring the status quo. The wealthy also tend to be older, and that leads to conservatism as well. Prosperous Southern cities—New Orleans, Mobile, and Augusta—voted for the moderate, Bell. It is truly a complex issue. As to Maryland, one historian has observed, "The Whigs of Maryland, as in many other Southern states, found their chief support among the planter class. These resided mostly in the Tidewater region."[24]

How did Marylanders vote? Let us examine the statistics for Maryland using the official returns of the election of 1860 (Table 2) and data from the census of 1860 as well as the election returns of 1860 (Table 3). From Table 2, it can be safely concluded:

(1) In Maryland, the election was a two-way race between the candidate of the extremist South, John Breckinridge, and the candidate of the moderate South, John Bell. Together they garnered 91 percent of the vote.

(2) Breckinridge, the candidate of the extremist South, did very well in Maryland. He polled 45.9 percent of the popular vote and narrowly carried the state in the winner-take-all elec-

tion. However, he carried only Baltimore City and five out of twenty-one counties;

(3) Bell, the candidate of the moderate South, also did very well. He polled 45.1 percent of the popular vote and, significantly, carried sixteen out of twenty-one counties.

But who voted for whom, and how does it impact THE QUESTION? Interpretations of the election returns are numerous. As previously noted, historians have compared old party affiliations with the new parties of 1860; the vote from areas with large numbers of slaves *vs.* small numbers of slaves; and the vote of one geographic region *vs.* another, for instance Southern Maryland *vs.* Western Maryland. In this work, an examination of the election results will be made in an effort to understand Maryland's voting patterns and how they could have affected a vote on secession.

The numbers seem to support the notion that Bell, not Breckinridge, should have carried Maryland in the election of 1860. As illustrated in Table 2, St. Mary's and Charles counties looked much different from the rest of Southern Maryland or the Eastern Shore, the most Southern parts of the state. They gave extremely wide margins of victory to Breckinridge while, for the most part, the rest of that region gave majorities to Bell. This can be explained in part by the heavy Catholic population of these two counties and Catholics' hesitance to support Bell and the Constitutional Unionists because of their anti-immigrant and sometimes anti-Catholic rhetoric. And Baltimore City, with its large commercial base and wealth, should have voted for the moderate Bell, as did New Orleans and Mobile, but because of an anti–Know-Nothing backlash which hurt Bell, Breckinridge carried the city. Bell almost carried the state and probably should have. Maryland then would have been in line with her sister states of the upper South, Tennessee and Virginia, which Bell carried. Furthermore, moderates ran most strongly in the upper South and, indeed, the Constitutional Union Party was formed in the upper South with many of that region's most prominent political figures counted among its supporters. Former party affiliation certainly played some role in determining voter preference for one candidate or another.

A review of the election results looking at counties with large numbers of blacks (free and slave) *vs.* small numbers of blacks; and at counties with large numbers of slaves (the counties with many large plantations) *vs.* low numbers of slaves, indicates a relatively consistent voting pattern. Table 3 illustrates—by county—the percentage of blacks and the number of large plantations relative to the percentage of votes for Breckinridge and Bell.

A close examination of the data presented in Table 3 reveals that Breckinridge ran as well in Baltimore, Frederick, and Washington Counties (with low percentages of blacks) as he did in Calvert, Montgomery, and Somerset (counties with high percentages of blacks). Interestingly, Bell carried all six of these counties. It was Bell, not Breckinridge, who carried the majority of Southern Maryland and Eastern Shore counties, where resided the greatest percentages of blacks.

The data illustrates the same point by showing the number of large slaveholders—those with ten or more slaves—and the percentage of the vote for either Breckinridge or Bell. In Maryland, as in other parts of the South, many counties with large numbers of plantations voted for the moderate, Bell. For example, the counties with the greatest number of large plantations or farms of some size (as measured by one hundred or more slaveholders with ten or more slaves) were Anne Arundel (265), Calvert (153), Charles (348), Dorchester (118), Montgomery (184), Prince George's (379), Queen Anne'S (138), Saint Mary's (236), Somerset (152), and Talbot (105). These ten counties, then, were dominated by the slaveholding oligarchy of the state. Exclud-

TABLE 3

1860 Census Data and the Election of 1860 in Maryland

Subdivision*	White	Slave	Free Black	Total	Black (%)	Breckinridge (%)	Bell (%)
Baltimore							
City (6)	156,622	2,218	25,680	184,520	15.1	49.6	41.8
Baltimore (80)	74,620	3,182	4,231	82,033	9.0	46.0	47.2
Carroll (9)	22,522	783	1,225	24,533	8.2	40.1	51.1
Cecil (16)	19,994	950	2,918	23,862	16.2	39.1	46.6
Harford (46)	17,971	1,800	3,644	23,415	23.3	43.0	52.4
Frederick (78)	38,391	3,243	4,957	46,571	17.6	43.3	49.3
Washgtn (22)	28,305	1,435	1,677	31,417	9.9	45.7	47.3
Allegany (11)	27,215	666	467	28,348	4.0	23.2	36.0
Anne							
Arundel (265)	11,704	7,332	4,864	23,900	51.0	47.1	48.2
Calvert (153)	3,997	4,609	1,841	10,447	61.7	46.6	48.1
Charles (348)	5,796	9,653	1,068	16,517	64.9	60.4	35.9
Howard (86)	9,081	2,862	1,395	13,338	31.9	34.2	53.5
Montgy. (184)	11.349	5,421	1,552	18,322	38.1	46.3	47.5
Prince							
George's (379)	9,650	12,479	1,198	23,327	58.6	53.0	44.8
St. Mary's (236)	6,798	6,549	1,866	15,213	55.3	67.1	19.0
Caroline (12)	7,604	739	2,786	11,129	31.7	42.8	49.4
Dorcester (118)	11,654	4,123	4,684	20,461	43.0	47.0	50.4
Kent (57)	7,347	2,509	3,211	13,267	43.1	41.8	51.3
Queen							
Anne's (138)	8,415	4,174	3,372	15,961	47.3	49.2	50.8
Somerset (152)	15,332	5,089	4,571	24,992	38.6	45.0	51.7
Talbot (105)	8,106	3,725	2,964	14,795	45.2	50.1	44.3
Worcester (79)	13,442	3,648	3,571	20,661	34.9	52.9	39.3
Total	515,918	87,189	83,942	687,049	24.9	45.9	45.1

*Numbers in parentheses indicate the number of slaveholders in each subdivision with ten or more slaves.

ing Saint Mary's and Charles counties for the reasons previously mentioned, Bell carried six of the eight remaining counties. It is also important to note that of 92,649 votes cast in Maryland, slaveholders represented only 14.8 percent, assuming that all slaveholders voted. The slaveholding oligarchy represented only 2.8 percent of eligible voters. Slaveholders simply did not have enough votes to dominate the election.

The data presented in Tables 2 and 3 demonstrate the striking fact that the radical Southern candidate, Breckinridge, did well in almost every part of the state. He ran as well in Washington County and Baltimore County in the western and northern parts of the state as he did in Anne Arundel or Dorchester, in the southern and Eastern Shore sections. Breckinridge did not fare better in the more southern-leaning parts of the state, at least not from a statistically significant standpoint. Bell carried six out of ten counties dominated by the slaveholding oligarchy and carried the vast majority of counties.

It is difficult to prove, categorically, generalizations regarding who voted for whom in the upper South. But in Maryland, no matter how one arranges the numbers—by former party affiliation, by region, by high concentrations of blacks—the central conclusion is that most nonslaveholding Marylanders voted for Breckinridge and many of the planter class for Bell, much like the pattern in the seceding states of the upper South. Breckinridge, the candidate of the extremist South, ran well throughout the state; Bell, the candidate of the moderate South, did likewise. Marylanders overwhelmingly rejected the Northern candidates, Lincoln and Douglas, in their last free election before the war.

Finally, an additional comment must be made regarding the question of race, because understanding the race question helps explain why Maryland probably would have seceded and joined the Southern Confederacy. Marylanders of 1860, whether great slaveowner or the nonslaveholder of modest means, were concerned primarily with the issue of how to manage large numbers of freed slaves. Maryland had led the nation in the manumission of slaves (the formal process of granting slaves freedom) and by 1860 the number of freed blacks nearly matched the number of slaves, 83,942 free to 87,189 slave. Maryland also led in novel ways in addressing the problem. In 1831 the Maryland Colonization Society formed to return free blacks to settlements in Liberia on the west coast of Africa, efforts supported through annual appropriations by the legislature. But the number of free blacks continued to rise, eliciting concern from the legislature (and the white citizenry as well). Marylanders recognized by the 1850s that the state's attempt to colonize blacks in Africa had failed to decrease the state's black population, and some now concluded that blacks should choose between returning to slavery or leaving the state. In 1859, Democrats organized a slaveholders' convention, chaired by James A. Pearce, Maryland's Democratic Senator, to explore the possibility of expelling free blacks from the state altogether.[25]

John Brown's raid on Harper's Ferry in 1859 heightened the sense of anxiety in Maryland and throughout the South, and brought the Negro question home to almost every Marylander. Democrats moved quickly to capitalize on this heightened sense of anxiety. They denounced the radical Republicans and abolitionists with renewed vigor and passed legislation to satisfy the demands of the electorate. Encouraged by petitions "to reduce the number of free Negroes presently living in Maryland and to make manumission more difficult," the legislature's Committee on Colored Population in 1860 "presented a comprehensive legislative program, designed to make it harder to be a free black man in the state. . . . manumission was prohibited, colonization and departure from the state were encouraged, free Negroes were legally entitled to renounce their freedom and choose their own masters, and be sold into slavery for minor offenses, and county commissioners were to register all free Negroes in their district."[26] These laws, directed at controlling the state's burgeoning free black population, were supported by rank-and-file Marylanders as well as the slave-holding oligarchy. This was a very real issue at the time. Marylanders recoiled at the thought of Republicans somehow taking control of this issue, and it had a significant influence on the electorate.

In summary, three conclusions can be drawn from an examination of the election of 1860:

(1) The results clearly indicate that the nation voted along sectional lines, and Marylanders voted overwhelmingly for the Southern parties.

(2) Maryland voted identically to the upper South. She voted similar to the South in her support for Breckinridge, the extremist Southern candidate; in her support for Bell, the moderate Southern candidate; and, in her almost total rejection of the Northern candidates, whether the moderate Douglas or the extremist Lincoln.

(3) Breckinridge and Bell ran equally well in almost every part of Maryland. As across the upper South, much of Maryland's slave-holding oligarchy voted for the moderate, Bell, and much of the non-slaveholding middle class voted for the extremist, Breckinridge.

The central conclusion relative to THE QUESTION is that Maryland voted similarly to the Southern states that chose to secede. On April 15, when Lincoln's Proclamation of Insurrection and call for troops to put down the rebellion forced Marylanders to choose, the fourteen thousand slaveholders of the state almost certainly chose the South. When their numbers are combined with the nonslaveholders, who tended to support the more extreme Breckinridge Democrats, this forms the large majority of Marylanders who would favor joining the Southern Confederacy. A suggested breakdown of the Maryland vote and the probable support for secession, by candidate, is as follows:

Candidate	Vote Received	% for Secession	Secessionists
Douglas	6,080	25%	1,520
Lincoln	2,296	0%	0
Breckinridge	42,505	90%	38,255
Bell	41,768	75%	31,326

Scharf and others suggested that approximately 20 percent of the Maryland electorate were Unconditional Unionists. This breakdown tends to support that conclusion.

A postscript is required relative to the Constitutional Union Party and the vote of the moderate Southerner, for it is important to an understanding of Maryland and the secession question. Many have assumed that the Constitutional Union Party was composed of true Union men in the South, but that is not the case. Old political patterns and allegiances did not disappear in 1860; the Constitutional Unionists were often defined by their unwillingness to cooperate with their former political rivals, who were now Breckinridge Democrats. "A close examination of the returns from the border states shows that the people voted generally in accordance with their former allegiances," argued Edward C. Smith.

> In the sections where the Whigs had always been in a majority—where politics was dominated by the slaveholding and commercial classes—the voter favored the Constitutional Union Party. On the other hand, the poorer districts, true to their Jacksonian antecedents, supported Breckinridge. A change in the popular alignment occurred only after the secession of South Carolina. At that time the rank and file of the Constitutional Union Party in the Borderland were about as likely to choose the side of the South as were the Breckinridge Democrats.[27]

This is the point: the adherents of the Constitutional Union Party—in the Borderland, in the upper South, in Maryland—"were about as likely to choose the side of the South as were the Breckinridge Democrats." That may not have been so after the secession of South Carolina, but it was definitely the case after Lincoln's call for troops to wage war on the South. The Constitutional Unionists were unionists, hoping for compromise and harmony, but they were also Southerners and states-rights men, concerned with the preservation and protection of Southern interests. "They opposed the Breckinridge Democrats in the election because the members of that party indicated a policy that would not allow time for compromise; but, unless compromise could be effected along lines satisfactory to the South, they favored peaceable separation."[28]

The Constitutional Unionists were strongly opposed to the federal government using force to coerce any state to stay in the Union, and obviously Lincoln's call for troops was not a compromise position, much less "satisfactory to the South." John A. Gilmer, a leading Unionist of North Carolina who was offered a post in Lincoln's Cabinet, feared that any use of force would unite the South. He pleaded with the Lincoln administration to avoid a collision at all costs. "There must be no fighting, or the conservative Union men in the border slave states of North Carolina, Tennessee, Missouri, Kentucky, Virginia, Maryland, and Delaware who are at this time largely in the majority, will be swept away in a torrent of madness."[29] On April 23, eight days after Lincoln had called for troops, E. B. Long entered this telling statement in his journal, "John Bell of Tennessee, lately Constitutional Union candidate for President, told a Nashville meeting he was opposed to the attempted subjugation of the South."[30] Bell was likely speaking for the vast majority of Constitutional Unionists, for they were Southerners, and they drew the line when it came to coercion or waging war on the South.

3

The State

The state for Maryland to watch, in regard to the secession crisis, was Virginia. Much larger and wealthier, Virginia's power and past gave it a special aura in time of crisis. "For reasons that stretched back over two and one-half centuries, Virginia occupied a unique place in both American and Southern consciousness. Home of the first permanent settlement in North America and incubator of the social system that would come to be called Southern, Virginia had been the dominant state in the nation during the revolutionary and early national period."[1] Without question, it represented a key state for the Southern Confederacy to have and to hold. In the late winter and early spring of 1861, Maryland secessionists closely watched the Virginians—for many felt that Maryland's fate was inextricably tied to that of Virginia.

Thus, before discussing the incredible days of that secession spring and summer, we must first discuss what occurred in the months just prior to April 15, because those events strongly affected the position of Maryland's secessionists. There is no doubt among historians that the secession movement in Maryland was very strong. William C. Wright stated: "The majority of Maryland's leaders favored one kind of secession or another."[2] Charles Branch Clark, wrote of the Southern Rights Convention Marylanders held in Baltimore in February 1861, "the convention expected Maryland soon to be out of the Union."[3] In a contemporary editorial, the *Baltimore Sun* asserted, "The people of the North . . . do not, perhaps, realize the fact that with the secession of the lower tier of States, that of all the rest of the slave States is inevitable. . . . If disunion proves inevitable, the line will be drawn North of Maryland."[4]

After the election of Abraham Lincoln and the secession of the deep South, a spontaneous movement began in the upper South, and indeed the entire borderland to seek a compromise that would restore the Union. "Taken as a whole, the Borderland stood, on March 4th, in an attitude of hopeful expectancy that measures would yet be devised to preserve the Union."[5] The dominant feeling in the upper South and Maryland at this time was to preserve the Union by finding a compromise that would be acceptable to both sides. Commonly heard in Maryland during these tense months was the phrase, "wait for Virginia, if she leaves the Union, so must we." Not only was Maryland connected closely with Virginia by an "affinity of institutions and industrial activities," but as it partially surrounded Maryland, and controlled the outlet of her water highways, "a feeling had long existed that Maryland's policy was necessarily bound up with that of Virginia."[6]

To understand Maryland's drive toward secession, we must first look at Virginia's secession movement and the drama of the peace conferences. The obvious reason is that Maryland was imprisoned by her geography. She could not seriously consider secession if Virginia, or North Carolina, decided to stay in the Union, for that would have meant secession albeit in isolation from the rest of the Southern Confederacy.

In the spring of 1861 it was unclear whether Virginia would

secede. On April 4 the Virginia State Convention voted against secession, and various peace efforts continued right up until the firing on Fort Sumter eight days later. In addition, there was the matter of Washington, D.C., the nation's capital. Positioned on Maryland's border and opposite Virginia, its physical location became the trump card played against the secession movement in Maryland.

Two principal efforts to find compromise were made in the early spring of 1861: an elaborate measure introduced in the Congress by Senator John J. Crittenden of Kentucky, known as the Crittenden Compromise, and the Peace Convention, called by the Virginia State Convention in February 1861.

The efforts of the United States Congress to reach a compromise were exhaustive. Largely promoted by leaders of the upper South and the borderland, the compromise measures were generally regarded as thorough, fair, and accommodating to both sides. Some historians say they were especially favorable to the South. The congressional session held in the winter of 1860–1861 was "noteworthy chiefly for the tremendous efforts made by the representatives of the conservative sections to effect a compromise." In the Senate alone, moderates proposed more than fifty different measures, each designed by its authors to reassure the South. "The great leaders of the moderate parties—Douglas of Illinois, Pugh of Ohio, Crittenden and Powell of Kentucky and Andrew Johnson of Tennessee—were indefatigable in their efforts to bring about an agreement."[7] The Crittenden Compromise proposed in December attempted to protect the slave system where it existed, gave newly admitted states the right to vote for or against slavery, limited the power of Congress to abolish slavery in the District of Columbia and to interfere with the transport of slaves, and provided for compensation to slaveholders for fugitive slaves who found their way to Northern States.

The Crittenden Compromise was very accommodating to the South, indeed, and throughout the country moderates hoped that it would pull the nation together. Only South Carolina had seceded, and Unionists in the lower South put all their efforts into pushing for acceptance. But the situation was ominous. Few Republicans were inclined to accept the Union-saving compromise preferred by Southern Unionists. The Senate Committee of Thirteen, created to find a solution to the sectional crisis, quickly found itself deadlocked, unable to find a formula that could attract support from both North and South.[8] On December 28, 1860, the committee voted against adoption of the measure, seven to six. The seven negative votes were cast by extremists, five Republicans and two Southern Democrats. The Republicans, flush from their November victory, were in no mood for compromise. "Despite Unionist blandishments, hardly any Republican of stature would accept the Crittenden Compromise."[9] In fact, they were locked in a vicious battle with departing Democrats over control of federal offices and the substantial patronage they controlled. Following this defeat of compromise, the six states of the lower South quickly seceded: Mississippi on January 9, Florida on January 10, Alabama on January 11, Georgia on January 19, Louisiana on January 26 , and Texas on February 1.

While the states of the lower South were considering and passing secession measures, the Virginia legislature issued an invitation to all states to attend a Peace Conference in Washington on February 4. This conference revived the hopes of the moderates throughout the nation that a compromise could somehow be reached to preserve the Union. Most importantly, it had a tremendous effect on the upper South. There people staked everything on the success of the Washington conference, and the response of the Northern states to the invitation of Virginia produced a conservative reaction against immediate secession. As a result, very few advocates of immediate secession

During the secession winter and spring of 1861, Maryland secessionists printed posters and broadsides to promote their cause. (Courtesy Daniel D. Hartzler.)

were elected to the convention, and five days later, on February 9, a proposed secession convention in Tennessee fell before a popular vote of 69,000 to 59,000.[10] The calling of the Peace Conference simply stalled the move to immediate secession in the region. "The [Virginia] Unionists who devised the idea of a Peace Conference thus laid a clever and effective trap for secessionists, who found themselves in the awkward position of asserting that the state's peacemaking efforts were futile. The Peace Conference stratagem would pay Virginia Unionists dividends on election day in early February."[11]

Well should the Peace Conference have raised the hopes of moderates, for twenty-one states answered the call and sent representatives—only Arkansas, Michigan, Wisconsin, Minnesota, California, Oregon, and the seceded states of the lower South were not represented. Furthermore, the conference attracted many of the nation's most distinguished leaders, including former president John Tyler (who chaired the session), William P. Fessenden, Lot M. Morrill, David Wilmot, Reverdy Johnson of Maryland, W. C. Rives, Salmon P. Chase, Thomas Ewing, Caleb B. Smith, David Dudley Field, James A. Seddon, Stephen T. Logan and others. Additionally, the powers in Washington seemed to be encouraging the peace process. Stephen A. Douglas wrote a public letter claiming that "there is hope of preserving peace and the Union. All depends on the action of Virginia and the Border States. . . . Save Virginia and we will save the Union."[12]

The Peace Conference had as its centerpiece the recognition of states' rights and an accommodation with the seceded states of the lower South. Delegates adopted measures similar to the Crittenden Compromise, striving mightily to attract representatives from the seceded states and to hold the radical Republicans at bay, but in the end, after waiting for weeks, the lower South did not send a single delegate, and the Republicans, again

Another Maryland secessionist broadside. The reference to the "Spirit of '76" connecting the Confederate cause to the American Revolution was a common theme. (Courtesy Daniel D. Hartzler.)

not ready to compromise, refused to support the final resolutions. On March 2 the Senate voted against the recommendations of the conference, and thus ended the last multilateral attempt to reach an accommodation to save the Union. "The failure of the Convention is one of the tragedies of American history; yet in this failure the radicals of both sides rejoiced."[13]

The failure of these two efforts (and others) at compromise had real implications for the secession movement in Maryland. While it is fair to say that during this period most Marylanders were supportive of the efforts to reach a compromise (they reacted much the same as did Virginians and Tennesseans), it is equally fair to say that this period of delay put the secessionists of Maryland in a position where they could not have acted. They simply could not have seceded before Virginia did, and Virginia was leading the national effort to save the Union. Of course, some Marylanders genuinely opposed secession, and delay strengthened their position.

During this period yet another factor complicated the secession movement in Maryland. The state was in constant turmoil because of the open hostility between Governor Hicks and the Maryland legislature, which had the support of most prominent state leaders. This bad feeling grew out of Hicks's election during the reign of the Know-Nothings (many said he was fraudulently elected), but it compounded itself when Hicks ignored the General Assembly at this momentous juncture. Hicks corresponded with other governors about a Border States Confederation without consulting the legislature, appointed delegates to the Peace Conference without their approval, and worst of all, refused to call a special session of the legislature or a state convention when a majority repeatedly urged him to do so. The purpose, of course, for calling the General Assembly into special session, or calling a state convention, was to debate and act on the issue of secession. In total frustration with Hicks, state leaders and members of the legislature held a mass meeting in Baltimore on February 1, where they denounced Hicks and called for the city and the counties to elect delegates to a state convention scheduled for February 18. Although this meeting had no legal authority, most Marylanders probably supported it.

The elections were held, delegates chosen, and the convention

Postcards like this one displayed Marylanders' pro-Southern spirit in the seces-sion winter of 1860–1861. (Courtesy Daniel D. Hartzler.)

met on the appointed date, with Judge Ezekiel Chambers in the chair. The opening paragraph of the first resolutions set the tone.

> Whereas it is the opinion of this meeting that in the present alarming crisis in the history of our country, it is desirable that the State of Maryland should be represented by judicious, intelligent and patriotic agents, fully authorized to confer and act with our sister States of the South, and particularly with the State of Virginia.[14]

Important state leaders participated in the Baltimore confer-ence. John C. Brune, president of the Board of Trade and member of one of Baltimore's most respected families, joined other speakers in "opposing coercion, blaming Northern aggres-sion for the country's present troubles, and underlining the point that Maryland's rights were even more important than the Union."[15] This was pro-secession talk, indeed. Note the tone of the resolution, "fully authorized to confer and act with our sister States of the South." *The lower South had already seceded.* Note, too, the *Clipper*'s report on Brune's speech, "Maryland's rights

A pro-Confederate envelope. (Courtesy Frederick D. Shroyer.)

were even more important than the Union." On hearing that Governor Hicks was committed to calling a special session of the legislature in the event the Peace Conference failed, and after completing its work by passing a series of resolutions, the Maryland Convention adjourned until March 12. The convention reconvened on that day, and the *Sun* of March 14 reported its resolutions on its front page.

> Whereas this conference, at its session commenced on the 18th February last, was adjourned to the 12th of March, in the full expectation that in the interim such action would have been taken by the Peace Convention, or by the Congress of the United States, or on failure of these, then by the State of Virginia, as would demand on the part of Maryland some decisive corresponding action.

But this extraordinary extra-legal effort to prepare the state for a decision on secession did not lead Maryland from the Union. Compromise prevailed, and the convention merely provided for sending delegates to Virginia while awaiting that state's decision on the greatest question of the day. President

Chambers was given the right to call the convention whenever he decided it was advisable, but it never reassembled. He did issue a call when hostilities broke out, but when Hicks called for a special session of the legislature, Chambers withdrew his order and declared that the mission of the conference was ended.[16] It appeared that Marylanders were indeed prepared to act on the issue of secession, with or without the governor's support. Most important was the decision of the convention to send delegates to Virginia and to await the action of that state in regard to secession. It also seems quite clear that Maryland leaders were simply not prepared to act on secession without Virginia first making a decision.

It is therefore crucial to examine the secession movement in Virginia in some detail. First, a caveat: there was a difference between how the term Unionist was used in the North and in the South. In the North, "Unionist" might well be preceded by "unconditional"—one who would preserve the Union at all costs. In the South it meant preserving the Union if accommodation was made to the South, and above all else, if the federal government repudiated the use of military force to coerce any state to remain in the Union. There were unconditional Unionists in the South, but they were a small minority.

Shortly after Lincoln's election, Governor Letcher of Virginia, a moderate and a Douglas Democrat, called the legislature into special session. By mid-January it had passed a law calling for a state convention and had set February 4 as the date for election of delegates. Of 152 delegates selected, only thirty were outright secessionists and about one-fourth were unconditional Union men, mostly from the Shenandoah Valley and the mountains. The rest, comprising more then half of the membership, were conditional Union men: they opposed coercion but strongly supported compromise and concession. Twenty of the total were

Douglas Democrats, 102 were Whigs, and the remainder secessionists.[17]

Thus dominated by Unionists (the moderates of the upper
South), the convention chartered a deliberate course and
strongly supported all efforts to promote compromise. Its leaders
led the Washington Peace Conference and it resisted the appeals
of the seceded states to join them. By mid-March the convention's Committee on Federal Relations had produced a report
that essentially recommended the provisions of the Crittenden
Compromise and rejected a resolution calling for immediate
secession. "The members showed a desire to remain in the Union
by ratifying a proposed amendment to the Constitution prohib-
iting the United States from interfering with slavery in the States,
and by calling a convention of the border slave States to meet in
Frankfort [Kentucky] in May."[18] The secessionists tested their
strength by introducing a motion to draw up an ordinance of
secession in early April but it failed by a vote of 88 to 45.

The deliberations of the Virginia State Convention were
watched closely throughout the upper South, but nowhere more
closely than in Maryland. When the Virginia Union men won
the upper hand, their victory had important consequences
north of the Potomac. Had the vote gone the other way, in favor
of secession, other border states might have followed, probably
including Maryland. But the Unionist victory served to check
the secessionist movement on the border, confining it for the
time being to the lower South.[19]

The following chronology helps to clarify the importance of
the Virginia State Convention relative to the secession movement in Maryland.

Virginia
Feb. 13—The Virginia State Convention convenes in Rich-

mond and proceeds to promote compromise and reject secession. It adopts resolutions opposing coercion.

Maryland

Feb. 18—The Maryland State Conference Convention, composed of many of the leading men of the state, convenes in Baltimore. After hearing that the governor "has it in contemplation to recommend by proclamation" the calling of a formal State Convention in the event of a failure by the Peace Conference now in session in Washington, it adjourns until March 12, unless Virginia passes an ordinance of secession, in which case the convention was to immediately reconvene. Also, it passes resolutions opposed to coercion and states that Maryland "should act with Virginia in this crisis."

Virginia

March 14–15—The Virginia Convention's Committee on Federal Relations essentially recommends adoption of the Crittenden Compromise and, again, rejects secession.

Maryland

March 12–14—The State Conference Convention reconvenes, passes a set of compromise resolutions, approves the sending of delegates to Virginia, and decides to await Virginia's action in regard to secession.

Virginia

April 4—Presented with a motion to draw up an ordinance of secession, the convention instead readily defeats it, 88 to 45. Lincoln sends an emissary to Richmond to arrange a meeting with delegates of the convention in Washington.

April 8—The Virginia State Convention sends a committee to Washington to confer with Lincoln in an effort to find some sort of acceptable compromise.

Maryland

April 8—The State Conference Convention remains adjourned, awaiting action of the Virginia State Convention.

Elsewhere

April 12—General Beauregard, in Charleston harbor, gives the order to open fire on Fort Sumter.

April 13—Lincoln responds to the Virginia commissioners by stating, "I shall to the extent of my ability repel force by force." This, of course, means the use of military force.

April 15—Lincoln issues a Proclamation of Insurrection and calls for troops to suppress it.

Virginia

April 17—The State Convention passes an ordinance of secession 88 to 55, and sets the date for the popular referendum on it for May 23.[20]

Maryland

April 20—President Chambers issues his call for the assembling of the Maryland State Convention but countermands it on the twenty-fourth when Governor Hicks finally calls the legislature into special session.

April 22—Governor Hicks calls for a special session of the legislature to meet on April 26 in Annapolis.

April 26—The legislature convenes in Frederick because Annapolis is already occupied by federal troops and the next day issues an "Address to the People of Maryland" which states that the legislature does not have the right to consider an ordinance of secession.

☆

Some historians and many participants in these events felt that the majority of Marylanders favored casting their lot with the South if the Union could not be kept together. After the fact, that is probably impossible to determine. What does seem clear, however, is the pronounced attitude on the part of Maryland's secessionists to wait for Virginia, an inclination that had the greatest impact on the secession movement in Maryland, as the events after April 15 so aptly demonstrated.

4

The Month

The despot's heel is on thy shore, Maryland!
His torch is at thy temple door, Maryland!
Avenge the patriotic gore,
That flecked the streets of Baltimore,
And be the battle-queen of yore,
Maryland! My Maryland!

James Ryder Randall

Since the beginning of the republic no single month matched, for pure dramatics, April 1861. A United States fort in Charleston harbor came under fire from erstwhile citizens. Lincoln called on the states for troops, a heretofore unimaginable event had occurred. The nation had gone to war with itself. It was the 2,725th month of Maryland's existence—March 1634, is generally viewed as the beginning of the state as a colony—and it would prove to be not only the most dramatic but the most pivotal month in its history. Maryland began April in a state of unprecedented anxiety, witnessed a bloody confrontation with troops in the streets of Baltimore, and ended it as occupied territory. Without question, the month's events determined the course of the secession movement in Maryland. This chapter will examine that brief period to illustrate why Marylanders and their legislature acted as they did. Events are pre-

Thomas Holliday Hicks, governor of Maryland during the fateful year 1861. His weakness when events demanded bold leadership drew the hatred of Maryland secessionists, who called him timid and threatened his life. (Library of Congress.)

sented as they occurred but are couched in a way to show how a Maryland secessionist probably would have viewed them.[1]

Many factors contributed to the defeat of the secession movement in Maryland. The gradual failure of the various compromise movements, the strength of the Unionists in Virginia and their influence on the Maryland Convention, the sudden action by Lincoln in response to Fort Sumter, the overwhelming response by Northern states to Lincoln's call for troops, and the speed with which they responded to defend Washington all had a profound impact on the legislature and the people of the state. Earlier the legislature had made its position clear, framing and adopting resolutions that expressed indignation at the methods pursued by antislavery forces but at the same time stating a determination "to cling to the Union" as long as its great principles could be preserved. The General Assembly had also expressed its "deep and solemn conviction that the Union must be torn in fragments" unless Southern rights were respected. The legislature had also assured "our brethren of South Carolina, that should the hour ever arrive when the Union must be dissolved, Maryland will cast her lot with her sister states of the South and abide their fortune to the fullest extent."[2] With the Maryland legislature clearly on record, then, here are the incredible events of April 1861.

The month began in Maryland with all concerned about the fate of the nation and most still hopeful that a compromise could be worked out to save it. On April 3, while Lincoln's cabinet was meeting to discuss the looming crisis at Fort Sumter, Marylanders learned that Allan B. Magruder had been dispatched from Washington to Richmond to arrange a meeting between Lincoln and the Virginia State Convention. On April 4, Lincoln held a secret meeting with John B. Baldwin, a prominent Virginia Unionist. Baldwin pleaded with Lincoln not to try to re-supply Fort Sumter. He also asked the president to call a national convention to settle the secession crisis and to continue to pursue a hands-off policy. But Baldwin's interview came too late—Lincoln had already decided to reenforce Sumter. On that same day, however, the Virginia State Convention, believing that Lincoln was following a policy of reconciliation, voted overwhelmingly to reject an ordinance of secession. Marylanders were in constant touch with the Virginians and monitored their actions closely.

The next day, April 5, federal forces evacuated another fort in the new Confederacy, Fort Quitman in Texas, reinforcing the view of many upper South moderates that Lincoln was, indeed, trying to find a way to restore the Union peacefully. In fact Lincoln had no choice but to abandon forts he could not reenforce with troops or supplies. The *Baltimore Sun* reported, "the Southern Commissioners, now at Washington, have telegraphed that they are of the opinion that the Cabinet will decide upon peace and a speedy recognition of the Confederate States."[3] Reports like these disarmed secessionists in Maryland and the rest of the upper South as well. However, the Lincoln administration was moving in a determined direction at this point—a direction that would risk war.

On April 6, Lincoln sent a messenger to Charleston to inform the governor of South Carolina that an effort would be made to resupply Ft. Sumter, thus setting forth a more aggressive policy toward retaining federal property in the seceded states. Lincoln felt he must act firmly, for his cabinet and the Northern press were pressuring him to do so. Did Lincoln ever support compromise? It is a difficult question. In January he had written a confidential letter to Pennsylvania congressman James Hale in which he protested against any "surrender to those we have beaten," claiming that it would be, "the end of us . . . and of the government."[4] But Lincoln did continue to meet with Virginia's Unionists—why he did so is open to speculation.

On Sunday, April 7, Lincoln met with John M. Botts, another prominent Virginia Unionist and former congressman, and thus kept active the perception that compromise was possible. Though all efforts at compromise had failed, Marylanders and indeed moderate men throughout the South clung, perhaps unrealistically, to their belief that Lincoln was bargaining in good faith and that the Union eventually would be preserved. Indeed, the very continuation of the various peace efforts reenforced those beliefs.[5] But public perception and the reality of the situation were rapidly diverging. "The fate of southern Unionism was sealed by decisions made in late March and early April. Lincoln concluded that he must try to achieve reunion in a manner the [Southern] Unionists considered catastrophic. All that remained was for the consequences of his decision to unfold."[6]

Again note the critical role played by Virginia. Maryland's State Convention had met and decided to act with Virginia. Ambrose R. Wright, Georgia's representative to the Maryland Convention, observed that while Marylanders "thought the cotton States had acted with undue haste and precipitancy" they were "almost unanimous for resistance to Black Republican rule, and determined to cooperate with the seceding States in the event that Virginia should determine to withdraw from the Federal Government." Wright also noted that "however mortifying it may be to her gallant sons," geography compelled Maryland "to direct her action in concert with Virginia, that State and North Carolina lying immediately between her and the cotton States."[7] Baltimore's Mayor George Brown, who also attended the convention, wrote after the war that Maryland's sympathies, though divided between North and South, had "a decided preponderance on the Southern side." Like several other states, Maryland anxiously watched as Virginia's convention, dominated by delegates favoring the Union, considered the "momentous question of union or secession."[8] And finally, William Wilkens Glenn, owner of the pro-Southern *Baltimore Daily Exchange*, wrote:

> The Peace Convention met in Washington and dispersed without effecting anything. Every one saw matters were getting worse daily and still nobody in Maryland at least dreamed of the terrible revolution into which we were drifting. What astonished me most was that there were no leaders in Maryland who were willing to take a prominent part or act independently. There was but one opinion. Everyone said "Wait for Virginia. See what she does." Even Mr. Norris [William Norris, a leader of Baltimore's radical secessionists] and his party who were extreme enough for anything insisted on waiting for Virginia.[9]

The Virginia Convention on April 4 had voted against a motion to draw up an ordinance of secession by almost two to one. In addition, on April 8 the Virginia State Convention dispatched a committee to Washington to confer with Lincoln on the next steps for the reconciliation process. Lincoln had concealed his real purpose to the public, and the Unionists of the upper South were still pursuing peace. "Virginia Unionists thought the situation under control and had little sense of working against a deadline. Believing that peacekeeping and reunion would be a protracted process, they acted deliberately."[10] So the first week of April ended with the Maryland Convention recessed and the Virginia State Convention voting strongly against secession and about to send delegates to confer with Lincoln.

A digression is necessary here to discuss just what bound Southerners of the day together. This was a period of great divisiveness and, indeed, confusion in the country, particularly in the upper South with its majority of pro-Union moderates and a large minority of radical secessionists. But as previously mentioned, most historians concede there were two issues on which Southerners were in almost unanimous agreement: distrust, even hatred, of the Republican Party, and a thorough opposition to the use of force by the federal government to coerce any state to stay in the Union. The absence of votes in the South for the Republican Party in the presidential election of 1860 is ample evidence of the former. "The real fact is that there is no good feeling in the South toward the present administration as such and very little toward even the Democracy of the North."[11] Two noted Maryland historians commented on these issues. Radcliffe, in speaking of the sense of Marylanders in April, wrote:

> Yet there was a marked hesitation, except on the part of a very small minority, to urge instant secession, though perhaps the larger number of people in the state believed that of the two divisions, which seemed inevitable, Maryland would in time go with the Southern. Whatever differences of opinion existed among the people of the state, on one point they were practically united, and that was in opposition to the aims and principles of the Republican Party.[12]

Scharf, in addressing the issue of coercion, stated:

> While four-fifths of the people of Maryland at this time regarded the course which had been adopted by the cotton States as rash, hasty, unadvised and uncalled for, yet there was one point upon which we believe the people of this State were almost unanimous, and that was against the idea of coercing the Southern States by the physical power of the Federal government or the northern people.[13]

Whether these comments truly reflect the general feeling in Maryland at this time is difficult to document. William Wilkens Glenn described the tormented mind of Marylanders at a meeting of prominent Baltimoreans. "One and all expressed the same sentiment. 'We are for the Union first. If that cannot be saved, then we are for the South.' They were all men engaged in business, strongly inclined to regard their own interests and evidently not at all disposed to revolutionizing."[14] The moderate and radical Marylander, and men throughout the upper South, came together on these two issues—issues that were about to break upon the upper South.

April 8 found Lincoln still in consultation with Virginia's Unionists (on this day a formal delegation from the Virginia State Convention was on its way to see him), and some real confusion existed regarding his policy toward Fort Sumter. Secretary of State William H. Seward, the acknowledged leader of the moderate faction of the Republican Party, in conferring with the Confederate commissioners sent to Washington, had, rightly or wrongly, informed them that Sumter would be evacuated—and they had sent such word to the authorities in South Carolina. The administration had created the impression that by evacuating the fort the federal government was setting a policy to avoid precipitating a crisis.

On April 9, however, the ship *Baltic* set sail from New York for Charleston, with Lincoln's personnel emissary Gustavus V. Fox (later Lincoln's assistant secretary of the Navy who planned the blockade of Southern ports) on board with orders to re-provision Fort Sumter. In Charleston, General P. G. T. Beauregard placed his troops on full alert.

April 10, that fateful day, Beauregard received orders from Confederate Secretary of War Leroy P. Walker. In the event an attempt was made to re-supply Fort Sumter, Beauregard was to "at once demand its evacuation, and if this is refused proceed, in such manner as you may determine, to reduce it." This was, perhaps, the worst decision the Confederate government made in the early moments of the crisis, for in ordering Beauregard "to reduce" Sumter, it established the South as the aggressor and aroused the North in one great rush against it. After all, Fort Sumter was not going anywhere and certainly posed no serious threat to Charleston since it could be bypassed by commercial shipping.

On April 11, the last day of peace, Beauregard and Major Robert Anderson, commanding the garrison, tried to find some way to avoid the outbreak of hostilities. Governor Hicks met with Lincoln to urge moderation, explaining that the situation in Maryland was such that if Virginia seceded, Maryland might well join her. Thus, Hicks reenforced to Lincoln the view of his cabinet and most of the Northern press that Maryland was a serious problem.

On April 12 the war began. After failing to find a way to evacuate Fort Sumter, Major Anderson received notice at 3:20 A.M.: "Sir: By authority of Brigadier General Beauregard, commanding the Provisional Forces of the Confederate States, we have the honor to notify you that he will open the fire of his batteries on Fort Sumter in one hour after this time." He did. Meanwhile, the delegation from the Virginia State Convention, delayed by bad weather, arrived in Washington.

The next day Fort Sumter surrendered. Without provisions or sufficient ammunition, Anderson had little choice but to capitulate. Official notification was not immediately received in Washington, although word had reached the capital that Sumter was under attack. Lincoln met with the delegation from the Virginia State Convention and took a somewhat tougher stand by pledging to "hold, occupy, and possess, the property, and places belonging to the Government." Later that day, the *Baltimore Sun* blared, "Bombardment of Ft. Sumter."

On April 14 confirmation reached Washington that Sumter had fallen. Lincoln immediately summoned his cabinet, and they approved his call for 75,000 troops. Senator Stephen A. Douglas, attempting to rally Northern Democrats to the cause, gave his unqualified support to Lincoln. The Virginia delegates returned to Richmond. The second week of the month ended with a terrific shock. The Confederates fired on Fort Sumter—it surrendered, and thereby the issue was joined. Word spread like wildfire and jolted moderate men of Virginia and Maryland. What next for the upper South?

The third week of April can best be described as one of spontaneous combustion. On Monday, April 15, Lincoln electrified the nation by issuing his Proclamation of Insurrection and his call for 75,000 volunteers to put down the rebellion. The North instantly responded with commitments to furnish troops. The states of the upper South, including Maryland, refused. The proclamation irretrievably divided the nation and destroyed all efforts at compromise. It played into the hands of the radicals, who now adopted a posture of righteous rectitude.

Moderates of the upper South felt Lincoln had betrayed them. Alexander H. H. Stuart one of the delegates to the Virginia State Convention, stated that he had inferred from his conversation with Lincoln on April 13 that holding the forts was the president's "specific purpose and that nothing like a general war was intended to result from the Sumter situation." He went on to say, without accusing Lincoln of "want of candor," that he was "so surprised by the appearance of the proclamation that he refused at first to believe it genuine."[15] The impact on North Carolina was much the same. Governor John Willis Ellis responded, "I can be no party to this wicked violation of the laws of the country and to this war upon the liberties of a free people. You can get no troops from North Carolina." In Tennessee, Governor Isham G. Harris proclaimed, ". . . in such an unholy crusade no gallant son of Tennessee will ever draw his sword." Governor Beriah Magoffin, in Kentucky, stated, "I say emphatically Kentucky will furnish no troops for the wicked purpose of subduing her sister Southern States."

In Maryland, Governor Hicks did not respond until April 20, and then he echoed other upper South moderates. He informed Secretary of War Simon Cameron that "the rebellious element had the control of things. . . . They had arms; they had the principal part of the organized military forces with them. . . . They took possession of the armories, have the arms and ammunition, and I therefore think it prudent to decline (for the present) responding affirmatively to the requisition made by President Lincoln for four regiments of infantry."[16] Lincoln's recruiting agent was told to leave Frederick immediately.

By issuing his Proclamation of Insurrection, Lincoln drove Southern moderates and radicals together in shared hatred and distrust of "Black Republicans" and an unbending opposition to coercion or forcing states to stay in the Union. The proclamation at once betrayed moderates of the upper South, who had firmly believed that Lincoln favored compromise, and indicated that despite Lincoln's assurances to the contrary, military force would be used against the Southern states.

In Maryland, the reaction was spontaneous and one-sided. Radcliffe, in classic understatement, wrote, "The call for seventy-five thousand volunteers by Lincoln on April 15, spread consternation in Maryland even among the 'Union' men."[17] Mayor Brown remembered, "After the President's proclamation was issued, no doubt a large majority of [Maryland's] people sympathized with the South."[18] But it was J. Thomas Scharf who captured the essence of Maryland's spirit.

> The call of the government for an army of volunteers created the most intense excitement in Maryland, as it showed that the government was determined to make instant and desperate war upon the South; and the announcement of the Northern press that Maryland was to be held by the North only served to increase it.[19]

Throughout the South the failure of Lincoln's April policy—the firmness at Fort Sumter, the call for troops after the fort was fired upon, and the proclamation of insurrection—served to alienate Southern moderates and conservatives. Saddened that compromise was not achieved, and conciliation not given a better trial, bitterly outraged at what they perceived as betrayal, those anti-secessionist elements at the South had no choice but to give way before secession fervor.[20] In Richmond the Virginia State Convention met at 10 A.M. on Monday, April 15, in a mood of extreme tension. Only the question of the proclamation's "authenticity" prevented the convention from going immediately into secret session. Unionists, clinging desperately to the hope that the document was forged, contended that "it could not be authenticated until printed in a newspaper Unionists trusted."[21] But the die had been cast—from this point on there would be no turning back.

Newspapers across the country shrieked with patriotic fervor. In town commons and squares Americans rallied in support for the Union or the Confederacy. The time for decision had suddenly arrived in the undecided upper South. The *Richmond Whig* took down the Stars and Stripes and put up the state flag, and Baltimore, Maryland's dominant political and commercial center of power, was ready to explode. Excitement was so high that Hicks received a telegram urging him to come to the city. He complied immediately and on finding the situation there critical went to Washington where he had interviews with Lincoln, General Winfield Scott and Secretary of War Cameron. He represented to them the intense opposition in Maryland to any attempts to secure by force the return of the seceded states.[22] Once again, Hicks alerted Lincoln and his cabinet to the pending crisis in his state.

On April 17, Virginia took the momentous step as the legislature passed an ordinance of secession. In Baltimore, amid rumors that Northern troops were headed for Maryland, there were pro-secession meetings and militia units were called to assemble. Governor Hicks, not a strong man to begin with and now extremely unpopular, drafted a proclamation to the people of Maryland (to be released on the eighteenth) that appealed for calm. That, of course, was impossible.

Compounding the enormous excitement accompanying secession and dissolution of the Union was Marylanders' awareness that for months their state had been the subject of anger and scorn in the North. The Northern press had long been suspicious of Maryland's loyalty to the Union. Many things contributed to the feeling—Maryland's status as a slave state, its strong reaction to John Brown's raid on Harper's Ferry, Baltimore's longtime reputation as a lawless "mobtown"—but none of these so much as the events of February 1861. Lincoln, on his way to Washington for the inauguration, stopped to make speeches at towns along the way. In Pennsylvania he was informed that a plot to prevent his inauguration and perhaps do him harm was taking shape in Baltimore. Governor Hicks himself had been given such warnings. "It seems that Hicks was alarmed by schemes. . . . much wild talk was rife. . . . the press in some sections of the country was . . . filled with lurid accounts of conspiracies existing in Maryland, and in and around Washington. The plans of the supposed conspirators continued to be delineated with a surprising wealth of detail."[23]

The plot supposedly involved certain Marylanders who intended to prevent the inauguration and even seize the capital. In any event, Lincoln, convinced the rumors were true, decided to go through Baltimore in the middle of the night and not make any stop there except to change trains on his way to Washington. Outraged Baltimore newspapers accused the president-elect of snubbing the city, thereby insulting every Marylander, and published rude cartoons of Lincoln and the incident, but elsewhere the reaction was far different. Some Northern papers were openly hostile toward Maryland and particularly Baltimore. When Virginia seceded, the Northern press reacted with still greater alarm regarding the safety of the capital, a development critical to Maryland and secession. Just prior to the outbreak of hostilities, Marylanders became the subject of assault in Northern newspapers, who now called for the subjugation of the state by military force and constantly urged Lincoln and his cabinet to take action.

On April 18, Baltimore was alive with activity. Governor Hicks issued his proclamation pleading for calm, and Mayor Brown did likewise, but Governor William Dennison of Ohio worriedly wired Secretary of War Cameron.

> We had made arrangements with the Baltimore and Ohio Road to transport troops, and Mr. Garrett was anxious to take them until late last night, when he declined, on the alleged ground that the Washington Branch will employ all his empty cars in transportation of troops. This looks ominous. We hope Harper's Ferry is safe.[24]

Virginia had seceded and her troops were rapidly taking up positions across the Potomac. Washington was a city obsessed with getting Northern troops to defend itself, and Cameron fired off a terse and threatening telegram to Hicks.

> The President is informed that threats are made, and measures taken, by unlawful combinations of misguided citizens of Maryland to prevent by force the transit of United States troops across Maryland, on their way, pursuant to orders, to the defense of this capital. . . . Such an attempt could have only the most deplorable consequences.[25]

About that time, four companies of the 25th Pennsylvania Volunteers arrived in Baltimore from Harrisburg on their way to

Washington. "As we disembarked from the cars we were surrounded by a hooting, yelling crowd, who lavished the most
opprobrious epithets upon us," wrote a member of the regiment.
Marching between two lines of Baltimore police while the
hostile crowd pelted them with insults, bricks, and paving
stones, the Pennsylvanians managed to reach their transfer
train. That afternoon, in a mass meeting in Baltimore, the air
rang with pledges to oppose any further passage of Northern
troops with armed resistance. To many a secession-minded
Marylander, Northern calls for the subjugation of the state were
suddenly very real. "When the Northern regiments came to
march into or through our State to the Federal Capital," Scharf
wrote later, "it was asserted that this was but a pretense of
protecting Washington, but in reality to secure Maryland to the
North."[26] Marylanders vowed to meet force with force.

The *Baltimore Sun* reported that Massachusetts and New York
were responding to Lincoln's call and that troops and artillery
were moving toward Washington. Hatred toward Governor
Hicks now reached its zenith. The governor suffered threats
against his life. His nerves shattered, well aware that militia units
were largely pro-Southern, and fearing that Virginia's vote for
secession might cause an outbreak in the state, Hicks secretly
wrote General Winfield Scott requesting federal troops if events
warranted. Cameron notified Hicks that troops would be furnished upon request. The Lincoln administration's policy to
subjugate Maryland had begun.

April 19, for Marylanders of the era, was a day to remember
forever. In the morning the National Volunteer Association, a
pro-Southern group of prominent citizens—not Baltimore's un-
ruly mob—met, presided over by T. Parkin Scott. Strong
speeches supported the South, denounced coercion and Lincoln, and urged preparation to meet the coming crisis.

Into this feverish excitement stepped the 6th Massachusetts

T. Parkin Scott, a member of the General Assembly, presided over a pro-Southern meeting in Baltimore on the morning of April 19, 1861, shortly before the Baltimore riot. Later classified as a dangerous secessionist by federal authorities, he was arrested without charge and sent to a Northern prison. (Courtesy, Frederick D. Shroyer.)

Regiment of Volunteer Militia, men who, in one of those remarkable ironies of history, came from Lexington and Concord, where on the same day eighty-six years earlier, another war had begun. To change trains the regiment had to be pulled in its cars from the Philadelphia, Wilmington and Baltimore depot on President Street across the waterfront to the B&O's station on Camden Street. Their appearance drew a crowd of excited citizens who blocked the tracks and forced some of the militia onto the street. As the soldiers marched westward on Pratt Street under a hail of bricks and paving stones, shots rang out, the troops opened fire, and soldiers and civilians fell in the first real bloodshed of the war.[27]

After the riots, another mass meeting was held in Monument Square where one of the city's most respected attorneys, Severn Teackle Wallis (in later years his granddaughter would marry the ex-king of England), denounced Lincoln and his policy of coercion. William P. Preston, another of Baltimore's most respected citizens declared, "I would prefer to die defending the constitu-

The Pratt Street Riot of April 19, 1861 sketched by Adelbert Volck, a staunchly pro-Southern Baltimore dentist. (Maryland Historical Society.)

tion as maintained by the South, than live a single hour under the fanatical tyranny of the North." Mayor Brown addressed the crowd, also denouncing coercion, and finally a timid Governor Hicks spoke, pledging, "I will suffer my right arm to be torn from my body before I will raise it to strike a sister state." Hicks ordered out the state militia and sent a dispatch to Lincoln informing him of the day's events, adding, "Send no more troops here."

Exhausted and still fearing for his life, Hicks took refuge in Mayor Brown's house. Also there were Brown, former Democratic governor Enoch Louis Lowe, Marshal Kane of the city police, and several others who had just learned that a large force was heading toward Baltimore from Harrisburg and had reached Cockeysville, a small community about ten miles to the north. Other Northern forces, they were informed, were massing in Philadelphia. The group agreed that Lincoln would not accede to Hicks's demand to "send no more troops" and decided to burn the railroad bridges connecting Baltimore with the North as the best way to avoid further bloodshed. They went to the bedroom

George P. Kane, Marshal of Police in Baltimore, heroicly set up a police line to protect Massachusetts volunteers during the April 19 riot and saved Governor Hicks from angry secessionists. In June federal authorities arrested him for being pro-Southern. (Courtesy, Daniel D. Hartzler.)

where Hicks was resting to get his permission, and most historians agree that he gave it, though Hicks later denied that he had. Whatever the case, men were immediately dispatched to burn the bridges. Their actions, construed as treason, electrified the North.

In Washington, tension rose with each passing hour. Lincoln ordered a naval blockade of Southern ports. He continued to demand troops to protect the nation's capital, but only a handful of Pennsylvanians were as yet on hand. Ominous telegrams began to arrive. From Harper's Ferry came word that federal forces had abandoned the town to Virginia troops. Then from Philadelphia, J. Edgar Thomson, president of the Pennsylvania Central Railroad, and S. M. Felton, president of the Philadelphia, Wilmington and Baltimore, two railroads charged with bringing troops to Washington, wired Cameron that there was resistance in Baltimore. "Having arrived at Philadelphia, we are informed by the Baltimore road that Governor Hicks states that no troops

George William Brown, mayor of Baltimore in 1861, attempted to prevent the attack on federal troops. Later he strongly protested the occupation of Baltimore by federal forces and was arrested and thrown into jail for his defiance. (Courtesy, Frederick D. Shroyer.)

can pass through Baltimore City; in fact, the Baltimore and Ohio Railroad refuse to transfer. We will wait for instructions." Next came the dispatch from Hicks in Baltimore telling of the riot and bloodshed. Washington, now cut off from the North, was immersed in rumors of impending peril. It was at this point that Lincoln and his advisors began to set in place the policy for the military occupation of Maryland, which, as it was implemented, kept her from seceding.

Cameron's terse reply to Thomson and Felton was heated but clear. "Governor Hicks has neither right nor authority to stop troops coming to Washington. Send them on prepared to fight their way through, if necessary. By order of the Secretary of War."[28] Lincoln and his cabinet had little choice. They had to secure the federal capital at all costs, for if the government lost Washington, it would quickly lose the war. Foreign powers and many of its own people would be convinced that the government of the United States could not quell what it called a mere rebellion.[29] To secure Washington, the federal army, what there was of it, simply had to control Maryland—it had to transport troops through Maryland, have full use of the railroads which ran across the state, and ensure that rebellious elements were prevented from threatening Washington.

The president, by declaring that Governor Hicks had no right or authority to stop federal troops from crossing his state and that federal forces would fight their way through Maryland if necessary, opened the issue of federal *vs.* state authority. Many Marylanders of the day thought they had the right to restrict federal troop movement across their state, and they were not alone. There were those in the North who supported this view. Abolitionist Wendell Phillips, in a speech at New Bedford, Massachusetts, only a few days before Ft. Sumter, agreed for completely different reasons. "Here are a series of States girding the Gulf, who think that their peculiar institutions require that they should have a separate government. They have a right to decide that question without appealing to you or me. . . . I maintain, on the principles of '76, that Abraham Lincoln has no right to a soldier in Ft. Sumter."[30]

By April 20 the railroad bridges had been burned and Washington cut off from the North, at least by rail. Telegraph communication was interrupted, adding to Washington's sense of isolation. Marylanders reacted to Lincoln's call for troops to wage war on the South as other Southerners did—they opposed it. "The telegraphic news from Baltimore to-day of the unarmed conflict of your citizens with armed Northern troops passing through to the conquest of the South, created a great furor," the *Baltimore Sun* reported from Frederick on the nineteenth. "The 'Union' gun is silenced here. . . . A vast change in the sentiments of the people has taken place, and nearly all stand by the South." From Annapolis the *Sun* reported:

There is great excitement here to-day. . . . The hitherto Union men are now crying out for immediate secession. Many are proposing to volunteer for the South. Cheers are given for Gov. Hicks for sending dispatches to President Lincoln to notify him that no more northern troops will be allowed to pass through the State. . . . The heretofore Union men are for secession—immediate secession and revenge. The old seceders are cheering for Gov. Hicks for sending his dispatch to Lincoln.[31]

Lincoln, was aware of the deteriorating situation in Maryland and acutely aware that the nation's capital was now surrounded by a seceded Virginia and a hostile if not soon-to-secede Maryland. He summoned Governor Hicks and Mayor Brown to Washington, "to consult with you . . . relative to preserving the peace of Maryland." Lincoln's real purpose was to buy time for federal troops to move nearer to Maryland—and nearer to Washington. Hicks spent the day alone in his room, trying to figure out how to cope with the rapidly changing situation in the state. Mayor Brown and some advisors arrived in Washington. Lincoln met with them and separately with Maryland's Senator Anthony Kennedy. The outcome of the meetings was agreement not to send any more troops through Baltimore but rather to bring them down the Chesapeake Bay by steamer to Annapolis.

It is very likely that the administration realized that sending troops through Baltimore would be not only troublesome but impossible.[32] On April 20 the War Department wired Major General Patterson, commanding federal forces in Philadelphia: "Send the troops now en route to this city by rail to Havre de Grace; thence by iron ferry-boat to Annapolis, . . . They should be prepared to march if cars cannot be provided. Carry out vigorously the orders of the General-in-Chief to occupy the road to Baltimore."[33] Brigadier General Benjamin Butler, who had just arrived in Philadelphia with the 8th Massachusetts Regi-

ment, was immediately ordered to Annapolis. He commandeered a ferry boat on the Susquehanna and arrived there late
in the night.

Meanwhile, in Baltimore state militia companies had responded to the call of Marshal Kane and other officials, and
troops were arriving by the hundreds. The city council appropriated $500,000 for defense. Preparations began immediately,
for it was feared that the city was in imminent danger. Two
members of Maryland's congressional delegation, Senator Kennedy and Representative J. Morrison Harris, went to Cockeysville, urged the federal commander there not to attempt to fight
his way through Baltimore, and convinced him to return to
Harrisburg. This undoubtedly prevented another major clash of
arms in the city. Northern papers reporting on the day's events
began to beat the war drum. The moderate *New York Times*
shouted, "A Day of Riot and Blood in Baltimore. . . . Pennsylvania
and Massachusetts Volunteers Attacked. . . . The Union Forever."

Lincoln permitted the Pennsylvanians to be ordered back to
Harrisburg, but by now he was desperate for troops to defend
Washington and needed time to organize their movements.
Other regiments would be routed around Baltimore. On the
night of the twentieth, federal forces abandoned the Norfolk
Navy Yard, turning over control of that important naval depot
to Virginia.

April 21 was not a pleasant day for Governor Hicks. At
daybreak he discovered General Butler and his Massachusetts
regiment anchored in Annapolis harbor. Addressing his missive
to "the Commander of the Volunteer Troops on board the
steamer," Hicks informed Butler: "SIR: I would most earnestly
advise you do not land your men at Annapolis. The excitement
here is very great, and I think that you should take your men
elsewhere. I have telegraphed to the Secretary of War, advising
against your landing your men here."[34] A governor telling a

military commander with troops at the ready to "take your men elsewhere" would have been humorous had the situation not been so serious. Butler, though, had come to stay. After the events of the nineteenth, Butler no less than the War Department for whom he was acting as agent considered Maryland hostile territory and was fully prepared to begin taking control.

Hicks had still another major problem on the twenty-first. No longer could he ignore the demands to call the General Assembly into special session. The governor had been under extreme pressure for months to call the legislature into special session, and events were quickly moving beyond his grasp. Secessionist leaders in Baltimore had informed him that if he did not issue the call, they would take the matter into their own hands. Glenn reported that on the twenty-first, "Doctor Rd. S. Steuart was in Baltimore. He followed Hicks to Annapolis & forced him to convene the Legislature. I am satisfied he would have shot him if he had refused."[35]

Meanwhile in Washington Lincoln had his own problems. With volatility in Baltimore and the railroad bridges leading to that city burned, Washington was completely cut off from the North by rail. Worse, the telegraph lines ran through Baltimore and were constantly interrupted. "Washington took on the aspect of a city under siege. . . . Business was suspended, stores were closed and locked, the streets remained empty save for hurrying patrols. At the first news of burned railroad bridges and attacks on troops, all transient dwellers in Washington wanted to go home."[36] Just a few yards across the Potomac, Virginia made preparations for war, and Maryland, which surrounded the capital on three sides, was erupting.

The messages from the War Department became still more urgent, more forceful, and clearer relative to the military occupation of Maryland. General-in-Chief Winfield Scott wired General Patterson at Philadelphia:

The direct communication by rail and telegraph between us is interrupted by many breaks between the Susquehanna and the Relay House, this side of Baltimore. . . . Please give your attention to the road up to the Susquehanna, and station a strong force at a point for the protection of transport steamers. . . . Major Porter . . . was sent several days ago [to Pennsylvania] to muster in volunteers, and to string them along the railroad in Maryland, leading from Harrisburg toward Baltimore. Please give your attention in part to this line of communication. Communicate frequently the arrival and departure of troops, numbers, and routes.[37]

Plans were being made to occupy Maryland as quickly as troops became available. General Patterson, from the headquarters of the Pennsylvania Volunteers in Philadelphia, wired Washington on April 21:

When we have sufficient troops and provisions, they shall be concentrated at Washington by means of the Annapolis route. The Government can take possession of the Washington Branch of the Baltimore and Ohio Railroad and the railway lines from Baltimore to Harrisburg, and thereby secure a safe and speedy means of communicating with Washington.

Northern regiments were given orders to fight. A message from the War Department to the soldiers about to enter Annapolis minced no words. "Take care to admonish the troops to be prepared, in landing, to repel force by force, as in war."[38]

The Northern press continued to scream for retaliation against Baltimore and demanded that relief be sent to Washington. The *New York Times,* in reporting on a mass rally in New York City in support of the Union, headlined, "The Entire Population in the Streets. . . . Over One Hundred Thousand People in Union-square." Northern volunteers organized by the thousands and moved south to save the nation's capitol—and south, of course, meant to Maryland. The *Baltimore Sun* began

Fired by news of the riots in Baltimore five days earlier, at New York's Tammany Hall the "Billy" Wilson Zouaves pledge allegiance to the Union and vow to "Go Through Baltimore or Die!" From The Soldier in Our Civil War: A Pictorial History of the Conflict, 1861–1865 *(New York, 1887).*

running regular columns entitled, "Latest from the North," "Movements in Virginia," and "Interesting from Washington." On this Sunday, the prayers of Marylanders were not answered, for Northern troops streamed toward the state, and in Washington plans were being made to occupy her sovereign soil. Thus ended the volatile third week of April.

The final week of the month began on April 22, when the military occupation of Maryland began. The 7th New York Regiment arrived off Annapolis on another steamer. Butler ignored Hicks's protest and disembarked his troops at the Naval Academy. He occupied Annapolis and began a troop movement toward the depot of the Annapolis and Elkridge Railroad, which ran to Washington. A detachment of federal infantry, with artillery, was sent to Fort Carroll to guard the entrance to

General Winfield Scott, the imposing commander of the federal forces at the beginning of the war. A Virginian and a superb military strategist, he clearly saw the importance of controlling Maryland and her railroads and planned the military occupation of the state. Scott was one of a very few who saw the prospect of a long and difficult war, but he suffered from the maladies of old age and was forced to retire shortly after the fighting began. (Library of Congress.)

Baltimore's harbor. Marylanders continued to react against Lincoln's call for troops, refusing to wage war on the South. The *Sun* reported from Rockville, "There is the most perceptible change in public sentiment in this community, in favor of secession, since the attack commenced on Fort Sumter, and the greatest satisfaction expressed at its capture." From Annapolis it reported "Nearly all persons in this neighborhood are now secessionists. The desire now is to teach the black republicans that the people of the South are not base submissionists."[39]

Governor Hicks at long last issued his call for the legislature to convene in Annapolis on the twenty-sixth. A delegation of Baltimoreans from the YMCA went to see Lincoln in an attempt

General Benjamin F. Butler, flamboyant Massachusetts politician and commander of the 8th Massachusetts Regiment. Given orders to bomb Maryland cities if the state seceded, he occupied Annapolis and later Baltimore, where he outraged Marylanders with his proclamations and disregard for civil rights. A Democrat, he had voted for Breckinridge in the election of 1860. (Library of Congress.)

to find some peaceful solution to the crisis only to be told, "Keep your rowdies in Baltimore, and there will be no bloodshed." On leaving, one of the delegates remarked, "God have mercy upon us when the Government is put into hands of a man like this."[40]

The War Department and General Scott continued making plans for the military occupation of Maryland. On the twenty-second, General Scott telegraphed General Patterson that ". . . [in] my letter to you yesterday I intended that the railroad via Harrisburg and York towards Baltimore was more important," but it is "of no value to us here without a force of, perhaps, ten thousand men to hold Baltimore—to protect the rails and bridges near it." He then began to expose his plans for Maryland.

"This shall be done as soon as we shall have a surplus force over and above what is necessary for the security of Washington." The message ended with Scott's bleak assessment of the mood in the capital. "Besides the troops supposed to have landed at Annapolis, we greatly need ten to twelve additional regiments for this place, now partially besieged, threatened, and in danger of being attacked on all sides in a day or two or three."[41]

The vulnerability of the federal capital and Maryland's favorable attitude toward the South was not lost on the Confederacy. On the same day, Jefferson Davis notified Governor Letcher of Virginia: "In addition to the forces heretofore ordered, requisitions have been made for thirteen regiments, eight to rendezvous at Lynchburg, four at Richmond, and one at Harper's Ferry. Sustain Baltimore, if practicable. We re-enforce you." Whereupon Governor Letcher telegraphed Major General Kenton Harper, in command at Harper's Ferry, that he was "hereby ordered to deliver to General Steuart, at Baltimore, one thousand of the arms recently taken at Harper's Ferry." At the same time, he wired the Governor of Tennessee: "The condition of affairs in Maryland and Virginia makes it important that we should know how far we may rely upon the cooperation of Tennessee to repel an invasion of our common rights. Please communicate fully and without reserve. Answer at once."[42]

In Baltimore a newspaper, *The South,* was established to promote the Confederacy and aid the secession movement within the state. Governor Hicks, in another of his hopelessly vain protests, asked Lincoln to withdraw all troops from Maryland and to cease all hostilities. The Northern press railed on. An article in the *New York Times* carried the headline, "Two Words for Maryland" and warned, "We shall preserve our right of way intact through Maryland . . . if the task needs half the men of the North, and all the artillery and missiles of death to do it. . . . We hold the fate of your State in our hands."[43] On the twenty-second headlines read, "Rapid Concentration of Troops at the National Capital" and "Troops Coming Forward from All Points."

On April 23, Baltimore City was in a state of great activity. Military companies mustered in and commenced drill. Arms arrived from Virginia. The city assumed a posture of desperate defense against the "hordes" expected at any hour from the Northern states.[44]

General Patterson reported to the War Department, "Captain Russell, of the steamer Louisiana, carried fifteen barrels of gunpowder, stolen from the powder-magazine at Norfolk, to General Steuart, Baltimore. Powder seized by police for the use of the mob. The Louisiana returned within an hour with cannon for the use of the rebels at Norfolk." In another communication he reported that, "I have reliable information that 8,000 men are now on their way from New York to Annapolis. Major Sherman arrived last night with his battery, and has been directed to take post for the present at Elkton, Md., supported by 100 infantry."[45] J. Edgar Thomson from Philadelphia reported to Cameron: "The suspension of intercourse between this place and Washington has caused an intense feeling here in relation to the safety of the capital, and there is great eagerness to rush to its assistance." In another message to Cameron he revealed sentiments that are perhaps representative of Northern feeling toward Maryland:

> Since I wrote my last of this date I have been informed that the Baltimoreans and Marylanders have destroyed the whole of the bridges on the Northern Central. This seems to have been a mere spite action, and must convince the Government that those loyal to the Government in Maryland are in a vast minority. As soon as the capital is safe from attack, it seems to me that the Government should at once turn on Baltimore and place it under martial law, and require that it should pay all damages to the railroads it has destroyed.[46]

More troops were ordered to force their way through Maryland to Washington. The War Department wired the commander of the Carlisle Barracks in Pennsylvania: "The Secretary of War directs that you at once order to this city and put en route the four companies of the Second Cavalry now at Carlisle Barracks. You will see that the companies are mounted and filled to the maximum standard, and fully armed and equipped for service. They will march from Carlisle to Gettysburg, and thence to this city, by the best route."[47]

In Annapolis, Butler took possession of the railroad depot and telegraph and began preparations for taking control of the railroad to Washington, a railroad owned by private citizens of Maryland. The *Baltimore Sun* of the twenty-fourth reported:

> Last evening the Vansville Rangers, of Prince George's county, intercepted a messenger from Washington, with sealed orders for Captain Blake, of the Naval Academy, and brought him before Gov. Hicks, who received the dispatches and afterwards handed them to Capt. Blake. It is reported that they contain an order for the troops to return home, it being impossible for them to cross the Patuxent. The Rangers report that nearly every man in Prince George's county is under arms.

An important point to observe here is that in these early days of the undeclared war, dispatches from Washington were subject to capture and telegraph communications were not secure. The plans for the military occupation of Maryland became known to everyone.

Lincoln's grave concern for the safety of the nation's capital did not lessen with the passing days, and his frustration at the arrival of no new troops burst forth when he shouted, "Why don't they come! Why don't they come!" In an article beneath the headline "The Position of Maryland," the *New York Times* stated:

Secretary of State William Henry Seward was regarded as a moderate in the Lincoln administration. In early 1861 Southern Unionists turned to him to save the nation. After the war began, many Southerners felt he had betrayed them. He was instrumental in organizing military arrests of suspected disunionists. (Library of Congress.)

There is beyond all question, a very strong element of rebellion in Maryland and Baltimore. . . . We now hold beyond question, the two great strategical points in the campaign—Washington and Ft. Monroe, at the mouth of the Chesapeake. With the command of the sea and abundant means of transportation, we can pour upon these two points all the soldiers we can raise. With 50,000 men in Washington, we shall see whether we cannot carve a way through Baltimore. . . . We shall make very short work of Maryland, when we have power sufficient to enforce our just demands. . . . We can in spite of her . . . crush any resistance she can put forth. We still hold the fort that commands her great city. She will soon be in a dilemma in which submission will be the only alternative to disastrous defeat.[48]

"More Troops at Perryville," warned the *Sun* of the twenty-fourth. The rapid and large buildup of Northern troops just to the north of Maryland's border (and even in some northern Maryland towns) caused great concern throughout the state.

In Tennessee, former Constitutional Union Party presidential candidate John Bell spoke for the vast majority of Southern moderates in stating his firm opposition to Lincoln's attempted subjugation of the South. This put the leadership of the Constitutional Union Party, the party which nearly carried Maryland, solidly behind the Confederacy. James Ryder Randall, a young Marylander teaching school in New Orleans who mistakenly thought a longtime friend had died in the April 19 riot in Baltimore, wrote a poem, *Maryland, My Maryland,* expressing his overwhelming anger and sorrow. Jennie Cary, and her sister Hettie, both of Baltimore, set the poem to music, and immediately it became popular with Marylanders and indeed all Southerners throughout the war. (Hettie Cary, known as one of the South's most beautiful women, would marry Confederate General John Pegram in early 1865, only to become a widow three weeks to the day after the ceremony.)

On April 24, Virginia, Maryland, and Washington were in utter turmoil. "The people of the counties on the Eastern Shore are making preparations for any emergency," reported the *Sun.* "The people are said to be almost a unit on States Rights, and will, when called, volunteer in defense of the State." Lincoln had been informed that the 7th New York Regiment had landed at Annapolis, but he knew nothing else. In fact, the 7th New York had its hands full. They moved out of Annapolis on the Annapolis and Elkridge Railroad to secure the railway to the Annapolis Junction, where it connected to the Baltimore and Ohio main line to Washington, only to find that Marylanders had torn up the tracks. Having armed the first car of their train with a cannon loaded with grape shot, they began to repair and take possession of the track. They arrived at Millersville in mid-afternoon, discovered the bridge burned to the ground—Marylanders had become quite adept at destroying bridges—and set about building a new one. Meanwhile, Washington braced for an attack expected momentarily. Lincoln was now near the breaking point. In speaking to the wounded men of the 6th Massachusetts he exclaimed, "I begin to believe that there is no North. The Seventh Regiment is a myth. Rhode Island is another. You are the only real thing."[49]

Lincoln had good reason to be dismayed, but the North was indeed rallying to his call for troops. Governor Oliver P. Morton of Indiana responded, "I tender to you for the defense of the nation and to uphold the authority of the Government 10,000 men." Ohio's Governor Dennison wired, "Your dispatch calling . . . for thirteen regiments . . . will be promptly responded to by this State." Senator Zachariah Chandler from Michigan wrote, "There is but one sentiment here. We will furnish you with the regiments in thirty days if you want them, and 50,000 men if you need them." From Illinois: "The Governor's call was published on yesterday [April 16] and he has already received the tender of forty companies. . . . Our people burn with patriotism and all parties show the same alacrity to stand by the Government and the laws of the country." And from Governor John A. Andrew of Massachusetts, "Two of our regiments will start this afternoon [April 17]—one for Washington, and the other for Fort Monroe; a third will be dispatched tomorrow, and the fourth before the end of the week."[50]

The North was mobilizing and doing it quite rapidly. Indeed, it was astonishing, for one must remember that in 1861 things took longer to accomplish, it simply was time-consuming to get people from one place to another when they were on horseback, walking, or at best, on slow-moving trains. The Northern press continued its relentless attacks on Maryland, Baltimore in particular, calling for the military occupation of the state. The *New York Times* announced, prematurely, "Martial Law Declared in Baltimore . . . The Business of the City Entirely Ruined." Alarmed at news that the president had consented to preventing troops from passing through Maryland and had indeed ordered a Pennsylvania regiment to turn about, the paper issued a stern warning to Lincoln.

> We will simply remark that the President runs no small risk of being superseded in his office, if he undertakes to thwart the clear and manifest determination of the people to maintain the authority of the Government of the United States, and to protect its honor. We are in the midst of Revolution, and in such emergencies the people are very apt to find some representative leader if the forms of law do not happen to have given them one. It would be well for Mr. Lincoln to bear in mind the possibility of such an event.

And this was one of the more moderate papers of the North.

The War Department nevertheless ordered the U. S. Naval Academy to move from Annapolis to Newport, Rhode Island. Marylanders must have been well aware of a tide of Northern troops moving toward their towns and homes, for it was reported widely in the press. It certainly was not lost on the legislature or on Governor Hicks. As Butler's troops took control of the state capital, Hicks ordered the legislature to meet in Frederick.

On April 25 matters improved for Lincoln—and worsened for Maryland. The 7th New York arrived in Washington late in the morning, the first troops to arrive in six days, since the bloodied 6th Massachusetts had de-trained on the nineteenth. John G. Nicolay and John Hay, Lincoln's secretaries, recalled twenty-five years later:

> Those who were in the federal capital on that Thursday, April 25th, will never, during their lives, forget the event. . . . As soon as the arrival was known, an immense crowd gathered at the depot to obtain ocular evidence that relief had at length reached the city. Promptly debarking and forming, the Seventh

marched up Pennsylvania Avenue to the White House. As they passed up the magnificent street, with their well-formed ranks, their exact military step, their soldierly bearing, their gayly floating flags, and the inspiring music of their splendid regimental band, they seemed to sweep all thought of danger and all taint of treason out of that great national thoroughfare and out of every human heart in the federal city.[51]

For Maryland the dam burst, and Northern troops began to flood over her borders in astounding numbers. Three New York regiments, the 6th, 12th, and 71st, had gone by sea and reached Washington by sailing up the Potomac River. The governor of New York wired the War Department that news of their arrival "has awakened emotions hardly to be described," and added, "Open the way through Baltimore, cost what it may." From J. Edgar Thomson in Philadelphia, Cameron learned that, "Matters are progressing here satisfactorily. We have ample provisions to transport ten thousand men daily from here to Annapolis, and I would recommend that no more be sent from New York or the East via the ocean. . . . The Philadelphia regiments have not yet gone forward, but I'm glad to say that General Patterson is using his best exertions to have them properly equipped, and will dispatch them as speedily as he can."[52]

In Washington, General Scott now began to put in place plans for the occupation of Maryland. Scott is credited with devising the Anaconda Plan for conquering the South—to control the Mississippi River and the Gulf and Atlantic Coasts and thereby squeeze the Confederacy into submission. In Maryland he implemented a smaller version. He notified General Butler:

> If this letter should find you not too far this side of Annapolis, I will ask you to consider yourself, for the time, as the commander of that city and retain a competent force to hold it. Next, I wish you to select a regiment . . . and string it at convenient distances all along the railroad, by the junction and

towards this city . . . to protect the road, its rails, bridges, and cars, so as to keep the communication open for troops and travelers between Annapolis and Washington by rail. . . . Send to this place all the spare troops from Annapolis as fast as you may find means of transportation, and report often.

At the same time, he wired General Patterson, informing him of his orders to Butler and instructing him that, "Sherman's battery, and a company of foot artillery with it, are needed here. If they can be spared from Perryville . . . send them to me. I wish Maj. W. W. Morris to take command of Fort McHenry. Perhaps he can only reach the fort by water."[53]

The plan to occupy Maryland was sprung—Scott appointed General Butler "commander of that city" and ordered him to "retain a competent force to hold it." "That city" was Annapolis, the capital of Maryland—the city where all the records of the state were deposited, where all the administrative mechanisms were in place whereby the state was run, and where the legislature met to do its work. Scott also moved to reassign highly respected military officers to key posts in Maryland, and what more important command than that of Fort McHenry, at the entrance to Baltimore's harbor? The federal military command considered Maryland enemy territory. To the military man, the terms "take command of" and "hold" implied the existence of a hostile force. Scott's plan was to surround Baltimore, the center of power in the state, and to occupy every other strategic point with overwhelming force. The *New York Times* headlined, "The Plan of the Campaign" and declared, ". . . the entire force of Pennsylvania should at once be thrown into Maryland for the twofold purpose of threatening Baltimore, and protecting the communications with Ohio and the West. . . . In good time, Maryland will be in our hands, and the refractory rebels at Baltimore put down." And under a headline, "Treason in Baltimore" it reported:

Simon Cameron, Lincoln's secretary of war, was a Pennsylvania railroad man who competed fiercely against John W. Garrett, president of Maryland's Baltimore and Ohio Railroad. He disliked and distrusted Marylanders, believing that the state was controlled by secessionists, and moved aggressively to subjugate them when authorized to do so. (Library of Congress.)

> We learn [by] key private dispatches from Baltimore, . . . that large numbers of leading merchants, and others, are, by words, if not by example, leading on the mob to their assaults upon Union men and Federal troops. . . . It is believed that the heart of Maryland, and Baltimore especially, are rotten and traitorous to the core, and that the majority of the first-classes have been waiting and preparing for months . . . to lead the mob against the real Union men and the Federal Government. Let no one now indulge in a regret at the probable destruction of Baltimore. . . . Let it be destroyed. . . . No compromise with traitors.[54]

Marylanders, alarmed and threatened by such reports, must have been truly concerned about the security of their businesses, their homes, and their families.

April 26 was the beginning of the end for Maryland secessionists, for on this date the order was issued to subjugate the state. Clear and unambiguous to all, the order is reproduced here in its entirety for, from this day forward, for better or for worse, Maryland would be kept in the Union.

Washington, April 26, 1861

Brig. Gen. B. F. Butler:

The undersigned, General-in-Chief of the Army, has received from the President of the United States the following instructions respecting the legislature of Maryland, now about to assemble at Annapolis, viz:

It is "left to the commanding general to watch and await their action, which, if it shall be to arm their people against the United States, he is to adopt the most prompt and efficient means to counteract, even if necessary to the bombardment of their cities, and in the extremest necessity suspension of the writ of habeas corpus."

In the absence of the undersigned, the foregoing instructions are turned over to Brig. Gen. B. F. Butler, of the Massachusetts Volunteers, or other officer commanding at Annapolis, who will carry them out in a right spirit; that is, with moderation and firmness. In the case of arrested individuals notorious for their hostility to the United States, the prisoners will be kept and duly cared for, but not surrendered except on the order of the commander aforesaid.

WINFIELD SCOTT.

It should be noted that the phrase, "if it shall be to arm their people against the United States," meant if the legislature voted for secession, for then, of course, Maryland would be in the Confederacy and, like Virginia, would go about preparing for armed conflict against the United States. So General Butler received orders to keep Maryland from seceding. And what an order it was—"adopt the most prompt and efficient means," bombard their cities, arrest people at the military's discretion. The order was not only dramatic but noteworthy because of the wide range of authority it gave a military commander in the field. Often in the history of warfare, these types of orders, i.e. use any means to accomplish the ends, resulted in some very harsh measures being taken by the military—a fact of which Maryland secessionists were no doubt well aware.

One week had passed since the riot in Baltimore, and the legislators had assembled in Frederick because Annapolis was occupied by Butler's troops. The legislature convened at 1 P.M., and Governor Hicks delivered a non-committal speech.

> The Governor's message showed that he realized the gravity of the situation. . . . there seems to have been a confusion in his own mind. . . . He had deemed that the occasion demanded the action of the legislature; yet he recommended really no policy to it on its convening. . . . He was not willing to urge an alliance with the Southern states, nor did he dare to inflame public sentiment still higher by advocating the rendering of assistance to the Federal administration. . . . He thought Maryland would be the probable seat of bloody war; from such a calamity he expressed his desires to see the state preserved.[55]

Northern newspapers that had heretofore supported Hicks now turned on him with a vengeance for calling the legislature and for proclaiming that no more troops should pass through Maryland. On April 25, the Philadelphia *Ledger* snarled, "Whatever the motives claimed for Governor Hicks may by his acts show that he is either playing into the hands of the secessionists or else weak in a situation where to be weak is to be wicked. . . . By his proclamation that no more troops should pass through Maryland . . . he has given countenance to the revolutionists. . . . His proclamation is an act of treason."

Hicks's life was still in some real danger. Radical pro-Southern men in the state were enraged at him for the sad state of affairs in which Maryland found itself. And a sad state of affairs it was. Annapolis was under federal control. Federal gunboats patrolled the upper Chesapeake, escorting Northern troops from Perryville to Annapolis. Troops were massing at Harrisburg and pressing into Maryland along the Northern Central Railroad while more gathered at Gettysburg, shortly to move on Frederick. Still other regiments were sailing up the Potomac on their way to Washington. Federal troops commanded Fortress Monroe, thus controlling the entrance to the Chesapeake, and from Washington troops had begun fanning out into Maryland to take up defensive positions and to gain control of the railways.

The *Baltimore Sun* reported almost wistfully that Maryland soon would be reenforced from Virginia and the South. It also reported that more troops had arrived at Perryville and Annapolis and ominously noted, "It is no idle want to say that within forty days sixty thousand men, thoroughly drilled, armed and equipped, can move from this point [Cockeysville] upon Richmond and Baltimore." The *New York Times* rejoiced, "A Flood of Troops in Washington . . . The Avalanche of Men and Money from the North. . . . Troops Concentrating at Annapolis," and shouted, "Clear the track, even if it should leave Baltimore an ash-heap." The various companies of Maryland militia were, for the most part, concentrated in Baltimore and totally unprepared to meet any large-scale invasion, which was fast becoming a reality. It was a wonder that Hicks survived. James R. Partridge, Maryland's secretary of state, fearing for his life, resigned his position at Frederick.

For the legislators now assembled, one thing must have been clear: Maryland was being occupied by Northern troops, and the state was powerless to stop it. All the members must have known that this would be the most important legislative session in the history of the state and that the welfare of her citizens, and indeed their very lives, might well hang in the balance of their deliberations. If Maryland seceded, there was "little doubt but that Northern troops would have compelled it to submit at once."[56] The secessionists of Maryland must have sensed the beginning of the end, for unlike Virginia and other states of the

South, they could not peacefully take action on secession—they were surrounded by federal troops.

By April 27, more troops had arrived in Washington, and tensions in that city began to subside. Lincoln and his War Department became more aggressive by the hour. They extended the naval blockade to Virginia, made several changes in the military high command to further prepare it for action, and suspended the writ of habeas corpus in Maryland. Most importantly, they locked in place the plan to occupy Maryland by dividing the state into three military zones, dubbed departments. From General Orders, No. 12. issued at Washington on this day, the pertinent instructions to the military were,

> 1. The Military Department of Washington will include the District of Columbia, according to its original boundary, Fort Washington and the country adjacent, and the State of Maryland as far as Bladensburg, inclusive. . . .
>
> 2. A new military department, to be called the Department of Annapolis, headquarters at that city, will include the country for twenty miles on each side of the railroad from Annapolis to the city of Washington, as far as Bladensburg, Md. . . .
>
> 3. A third department, called the Department of Pennsylvania, will include . . . all of Maryland not embraced in the foregoing departments. . . .[57]

If any doubt remained that the Lincoln Administration intended to occupy Maryland, the official correspondence from Secretary of War Cameron to J. Edgar Thomson in Philadelphia the same day erased it. Cameron began with a summation of the state of affairs affecting Washington.

> We have been without any response, except request for small matters of detail, while all my orders and wishes of last week

have been neglected. Until the day before yesterday we had not 2,500 men here under arms. Now we shall have enough in a day or two. The railway from Annapolis to this place, under the direction of Scott, will be open by Monday [April 29] for the whole amount of business of which it is capable.

Note his early frustration and his new-found optimism. But now, in vehement terms, he outlined what was in store for Maryland.

I have sent an engineer to reopen the Northern Central, and have ordered an able officer of this Department to take charge of the troops that may assemble at Harrisburg, and bring them in immediate connection with Baltimore, to be concentrated where the city can be reached. We must occupy it without delay. I will never consent, if the whole power of this Department can prevent it, that a rebel force shall prevent the passage of our fellow-citizens from coming here unmolested. The authorities of Baltimore have acted with bad faith, and one of the most painful acts I have witnessed was the order for the return of our troops from Cockeysville; but that is past, and now we will amend the error. The President has given me full power to open this communication, and I will do it.[58]

Again, note the clear, unambiguous message—"a rebel force" in Baltimore, "the authorities of Baltimore have acted with bad faith," "we must occupy it without delay," "the President has given me full power." It is important to remember that Maryland had not seceded at this point, but because Marylanders had acted in defiance of the federal government and were a threat to the nation's capital, the Lincoln administration adopted a policy to treat Maryland as if she had seceded.

From the field, Butler sent the War Department his longest correspondence to date. "I had the honor to receive this morning your letter from headquarters, of April 25th, detailing me to take command of this city." Note that it took two days for Scott's order to reach him from Washington. "I am deeply sensible of the honor conferred, and will endeavor to hold it." Butler now made one of his presumptuous statements presaging a boldness which would become a hallmark of his career. "I had taken the liberty to make dispositions for that purpose before I had the honor to receive your order." He went on to describe his preparations to occupy the city—Butler had turned the grounds of the Naval Academy into a staging area for his troops. Endeavoring to hold the high ground around Annapolis, Butler reported, "During the past night . . . the troops were disturbed by signal rockets being thrown up along the line of the interior road for some miles. . . . I have ordered an increased force . . . furnished them with signal-rockets, so that in case of attack we can immediately reenforce them from the academy." Then he gave an optimistic report regarding the progress he had made in occupying Maryland.

> We believe that we have entire command of the bay through the means of the iron steamers *Maryland,* mounting four 32-pounders . . . and the Philadelphia ice-boat . . . which also mounts four guns. . . . Acting according to your orders of instruction, I have sent forward the Sixty-ninth Regiment of New York . . . with directions to occupy the railroad from a point near the depot in Annapolis to the Junction. . . . It is believed that this regiment, being about 1,100 strong, will be able to protect the road and the telegraph lines from further depredations.

Next he reported on the expected arrival of reinforcements, "I expect the arrival to-morrow or during the night of upwards of three thousand New Jersey troops, some two thousand from New York and about one thousand from Pennsylvania." He gave an ominous assessment of the situation in Baltimore, "I have received what I believe to be authentic intelligence . . . that scaling ladders are being prepared, and that a force is being organized for the purpose of throwing up batteries on the heights, with the intention of making an assault upon Fort McHenry." Then he began to lay the groundwork for his troop movement on Baltimore. "The steam gunboat of three guns Monticello has just reported to me, and I shall be able to send up reinforcements or supplies. . . . Since I commenced writing this dispatch I have received notice from the roadmaster that the track is in good running order, but we are deficient in engines and cars." Finally, he acknowledged receiving the order. "I had the honor also to receive the order as to the course to be pursued in the case of the secession of Maryland. I will endeavor to carry out the orders with firmness and moderation."[59]

From the commander of its main force in the field, the War Department thus received the good news and the bad news. Butler had repaired the railroad line between Annapolis and Washington and for the most part secured it. Federal gunboats appeared to have no opposition on the Chesapeake, and thousands of new troops were expected momentarily. On the other hand, the rebels of Annapolis and throughout Maryland were still very active and posed a constant threat. The situation in Baltimore remained unresolved.

While the Lincoln administration was dividing Maryland into military departments and planning the immediate occupation of Baltimore and other key points, the legislature tried to conduct its business in the strange surroundings of Frederick. Moreover the situation was deteriorating daily—Annapolis was controlled by the federals; the Chesapeake and Potomac were patrolled by federal gunboats, essentially cutting off Maryland from Virginia; and Northern troops were massed at Harrisburg and Gettysburg only days, if not hours, from Maryland.

The legislature was acutely aware of its inability to control events in the state. The Maryland militia was undermanned, untrained and ill-equipped—they had some rifles, but little ammunition and few cannon. Given this situation, the legislators struggled with the issue of just what to do. Delegates from Prince George's County called for passage of an ordinance of secession, but this was quickly referred to the Committee on Federal Relations. The senate unanimously adopted as a resolution an "Address to the People of Maryland," which stated that the legislature did not have the right to act on secession and suggested that a sovereign convention would be called to consider it. Various bills were introduced to appropriate monies for the defense of Baltimore and the state, but no actions were taken that were directly hostile to the federal government. Maryland was defenseless, and every member of the legislature must have known it. The gravity of the situation was lost on no one. Scharf, a participant in the war and a postwar historian of Maryland, recounted it this way:

> Upon the opening of this session, intense interest was felt as to what would be its course in relation to secession. On the 27th . . . the Senate settled the question. . . . This resolution of the legislature greatly disappointed the wishes of a large number of ardent secessionists. . . . There was also dissatisfaction . . . because the legislature had neither reorganized and armed the militia. . . . the legislature could not . . . have possibly done a tithe of what some expected; and, moreover, if under the circumstances, it had taken any such steps, its rashness would have visited the city and state with heavy penalties. Any attempt to offer armed resistance to the proceedings of the federal government, would have not only resulted in failure, but in certain destruction of Baltimore. The State was in a more defenseless condition than it had been for years. . . . and before it had time to even consider the situation, the administration had already completed its arrangements for taking control of the State.[60]

April 28 was a Sunday, and from pulpits North and South rang calls for patriotic devotion to the cause and explanations for just and holy crusades. The New York East Methodist Conference opened with this prayer: "Grant, O God, that all the efforts now being made to overthrow rebellion in our distracted country may be met with every success. Let the forces that have risen against our Government, and Thy law, be scattered to the winds, and may no enemies be allowed to prevail against us."[61] For Marylanders, it was a time for prayer, indeed. The people of the North demanded their subjugation. Thomas A. Scott, who was now in charge of getting Northern troops to Washington, wrote Cameron, "You may rely upon it that action—decisive measures are necessary to satisfy all that you depend upon North of Mason & Dixon. Isolate Baltimore and subjugate Maryland—do it promptly."[62]

That is exactly what Winfield Scott intended to do, for on this Sunday he sent General Patterson a chilling—at least, if you were a Baltimorean—message:

> I hope in a few days to have the railroad communication between Annapolis and Washington well re-established and guarded, and in about the same time troops enough here to give reasonable security to the capital. . . . The next step will be by force to occupy Baltimore and reopen regular communications between Washington and Philadelphia by rail and wires.

He then proposed a plan for taking Baltimore.

> The plan that has occurred to me is, 1st, to advance a column from this place via the Relay House to the Washington depot; 2d, another column by the road from York; 3d, the same from Havre de Grace, if destruction of bridges be not an insuperable obstacle; and, 4th, to move the principal force by water from Annapolis, and to make the four attacks simultaneously. I wish you to consider and methodize the second and third

attacks, and give me your views in advance on the whole subject.[63]

The "Little Anaconda Plan" was now complete. Federal authorities had divided the state into three military departments and assigned commanders to each; the state capital was in federal hands; the state's railroads were under, or about to come under, federal control; its bay and rivers were patrolled by federal gunboats; and finally, its principal city, Baltimore, was about to be attacked and occupied.

A mere thirteen days had passed since Lincoln's call for troops, and but two weeks since the fall of Fort Sumter. What surely stunned each and every Marylander in April 1861 was the rapidity by which Northern troops advanced upon and occupied the state. The response of the Northern states to Sumter and Lincoln's call to arms was simply overwhelming.

—from Decatur, Illinois: "The war news creates great excitement here. A large and enthusiastic meeting was held last night. Several speeches were made by prominent men of all parties in favor of upholding the Government."

—from Burlington, Iowa: "Political distinctions are forgotten in the unanimous desire to support and sustain the Government."

—from Milwaukee: "An immense meeting was held at the Chamber of Commerce last night. Men of all parties participated and the excitement was very great. The feeling is unanimous for asserting the authority of the Government, and crowds of men are offering their services to the Adjutant General."

—from Detroit: "At an informal meeting of citizens today, at which Gov. Blair was present, it was resolved, in order to expedite the equipment of the troops required from

Michigan, to raise $100,000 by private subscription. A large portion of the amount was subscribed on the spot."

—and from Cincinnati: "The merchants have stopped shipping goods to the South."[64]

Marylanders must have been stunned by it all.

On April 29, a blue Monday for the secessionists of Maryland, Northern troops continued to stream across the state toward Washington. The federal command continued operations for the occupation of Baltimore and the subjugation of the state. General Scott advised Butler, "If Fort McHenry be not re-enforced, please send thither by some armed steamer from 250 to 500 men, with subsistence for at least sixty days." He then asked for Butler's comments on the plan to occupy Baltimore, "I shall be glad to have your views on my proposed movement upon Baltimore, particularly on the part to be fitted out from Annapolis, and which you will probably be required to command." Scott concluded by ordering, "A strong war vessel, to support Fort McHenry in case of an attack, is of great importance. If there be one not essential as a convoy to transports between Annapolis and the Susquehanna, send her to Fort McHenry." At the same time, Scott sent a dispatch to General Patterson in Philadelphia further defining his plan for occupying Baltimore,

> I gave you [on the 27th] the outline of my plan for taking and
> strongly occupying Baltimore, and I asked for your views on
> the subject. At present I suppose a column from this place of
> 3,000 men; another from York of 3,000; a third from Perry-
> ville or Elkton by land or water, or both, of 3,000, and a fourth
> from Annapolis by water of 3,000 might suffice.

Next he pressed Patterson for his assessment of how soon preparations could be completed for the troop movement on Baltimore.

When can we be ready for the movement upon Baltimore on this side? Colonel Mansfield has satisfied me that we want at least 10,000 additional troops here to give security to this capital, and as yet we have less than 10,000, including some very indifferent militia of the District. . . . The Secretary of War tells me that he has sent a party, not military, to repair the bridge and relay the Maryland part of the Harrisburg and Baltimore Railroad to a point near the city. This I am sure cannot be done without the protection of a military force. I wish you to look to this. . . . Tell me what you can do, and when, towards seizing and occupying Baltimore.

Scott ended this dispatch with a forceful postscript: "Occupy Havre de Grace at your discretion."[65]

Thus, plans to attack Baltimore continued to be made and towns in Maryland, indeed any points of interest to the military, were to be occupied at the discretion of military commanders. Of course General Scott was preoccupied with Baltimore primarily for strategic reasons. All railroads from the north and west to Washington connected through Baltimore: from the northeast, the Philadelphia, Wilmington and Baltimore; from due north the Northern Central Railroad; and from the west the Baltimore and Ohio. For Scott to transport large numbers of troops and supplies to Washington he must have control over the railroad depot at Baltimore.

In Washington the situation looked better and better. Telegraph communication to the North was restored, Butler swept westward from Annapolis, securing the railroad to Washington, and Northern troops continued to mass just north of the Mason-Dixon Line in Philadelphia, Harrisburg, Gettysburg and in Ohio and western Virginia near stations of the Baltimore and Ohio Railroad. Virtually all of Maryland's newspapers reported on these events. The *Baltimore Sun* had a regular front page column, "The War Crises" wherein it reported troop movements day by day. On this day, the *Sun* ran an ominous headline, "Arrest of Maryland Legislature," and reported, "We find the following, among other nonsensical statements, in the New York Times: 'Gen. Butler, commanding at Annapolis, says that if the Maryland legislature passes an ordinance of secession, he will arrest the entire body!'" If the legislators did not already know it, they were thus put on notice. In another equally ominous column, the *Sun* recorded the following dispatch from Harrisburg, Pennsylvania, on the twenty-eighth:

> The Governor's forthcoming message to the legislature will recommend the passage of a stay law. The declaration part will say that Pennsylvania will open a route leading from the North to Washington as essential to trade and transit. Whether Maryland stays in or goes out of the Union, no hostile soil will be permitted to lie between the capital and states loyal to the Union.

Thus, did Pennsylvania inform Maryland that it would wage war if the latter seceded, no matter what actions the federal government chose to take.

In Frederick the legislature continued to struggle with this state of the state and their own precarious situation. By a vote of fifty-three to thirteen they adopted the report of the Committee on Federal Relations, which declared the legislature did not have constitutional authority to pass an act of secession. In reality, it could not pass an ordinance of secession, for to do so would have precipitated an instant clash with federal troops moving through the state. Rumors of plans to prepare the state to defend itself were in the air, and some proposals were made. The legislature approved a loan of $500,000 to the City of Baltimore for defense preparations and asked the Ways and Means Committee to appropriate $2,000,000 for the state's defense. The *Baltimore Sun* noted, "Reports of a very large accumulation of government troops at Annapolis have reached here, but there is at present a disposition on the part of the legislature to offer them no molestation. The troops are reported by certain parties to have exercised very arbitrary powers by dispossessing citizens of their farms and property, which has created much indignation."

Marylanders must have seen the writing on the wall—their state was going to be overrun by Northern troops, and they were powerless to stop it. A *New York Times* editorial of this day stated:

> If it would be premature to regard the recoil of Maryland as in itself a material fact of much moment, but the lesson taught by the change of sentiment in that state is really a very valuable one. . . . Six days ago Maryland seemed wholly given over to secession delirium. Suddenly, by one of those swift veerings of popular feeling which resemble nothing so much as the capricious shiftings of the wind, unmistakable indications of a change of mind made their appearance. . . . There is no need of accounting for this change by any very recondite reasons. It is all owing to a little stern showing of the tusks of Power. Maryland, willing or unwilling, has been compelled to look in the face of the bitter dilemma forced upon her by an indignant nation—the free right of way for Northern troops through her territory to the National capital, or her speedy annihilation. From the latter alternative she shrinks aghast—that is all that the reaction so far, amounts to.

Enough said.

April 30th, was the last day of the month, but for Marylanders it would be the first day of four years of federal military intervention in the affairs of their state and their lives. Additional troops arrived in Washington, as the response of the Northern states to Lincoln's call commenced in earnest. The *Baltimore Sun* of this day reported, "There are about 15,000 troops quartered in New York, destined for Washington" and under the headline, "Increase of the Army and Navy" exclaimed:

The troops called out by the army and navy orders today are all additional to the seventy-five thousand volunteers already required, so that the whole number called for by the government thus far is: Volunteers by proclamation 75,000; volunteers for three years service 40,000; regulars for five years service 25,000; seamen for five years service 18,000—total 158,000.

So great was Northern patriotic fervor that on the thirtieth the New York Yacht Club offered its vessels to the federal government. "This was typical of the response of various groups, civic bodies, churches, schools, and other organizations who in their early-war fervor were jumping to the colors in whatever way they could. . . . the people were exhilarated by the war spirit, by the excitement, the anticipated thrill of the conflict—the grim awakening would come later."[66]

In Baltimore, "the grim awakening" was already taking place. With the railroad bridges to the north destroyed and federal troops in control of the railroads to the south, Baltimore was essentially cut off from the world. Business was at a standstill, food was in short supply, and the wharves were empty because federal gunboats controlled the Chesapeake, thus blockading the port of Baltimore. The awakening included still more threats from the Northern press. The *New York Tribune* commented icily, "So soon as everything requisite can be prepared and supplied, there will doubtless be a force of two hundred thousand men sent to relief of Fort Pickens, and it will march through, (not around) Baltimore, Richmond, Raleigh, Charleston."[67] To make matters worse, from Harrisburg the troops moved out on their way to Baltimore via the repaired Northern Central Railroad. The *Sun* reported on these events in Pennsylvania.

A requisition from the general government was received today, through the hands of Gen. Patterson, for twenty-one more regiments . . . making a total for Pennsylvania of thirty-eight regiments—twenty-nine thousand five hundred men. Col. McClure returned from camp at York to-night, and reports all right there, and the men eager to march through Baltimore. The people of Chambersburg have organized a mounted patrol reaching clear to the Maryland line. . . . Batteries of artillery are being formed at Chambersburg and other points of the interior, to protect any forward movement of the Pennsylvania volunteers.

In Frederick, matters were not much better. The legislature had decided to meet in secret session to consider Senator Coleman Yellott's safety bill. Yellott, a well-known secessionist, had introduced a bill to establish a wartime commission of seven members, including the governor, to run the state during this rapidly unfolding crisis. The commissioners were to control the militia and most of the civilian state government and had near dictatorial powers. All of the proposed commissioners were known Southern men, with the exception of Governor Hicks. Thus, the legislature began to move the state toward defending itself against the invasion of Northern troops—by sending monies to Baltimore to prepare its defenses, by moving to appropriate monies to arm the state, and by going into secret session to consider the extraordinary Yellott Bill. And if the state was going to defend itself it had to act quickly, for the invasion had truly begun. The *Sun* of the thirtieth stated:

An understanding has been entered into between the Governors of New York, Pennsylvania, Ohio and Indiana, by which those states shall act in conjunction to throw troops and provisions into Washington, or elsewhere South, upon orders of the War Department. . . . Wheeling in Virginia, and some point on the northwestern line of Maryland, are to be fixed upon for the concentration of troops.

The legislature was deeply concerned, if not frightened about

This 1861 map of central Maryland illustrates the roads and railroads converging on Baltimore and Washington from the North.

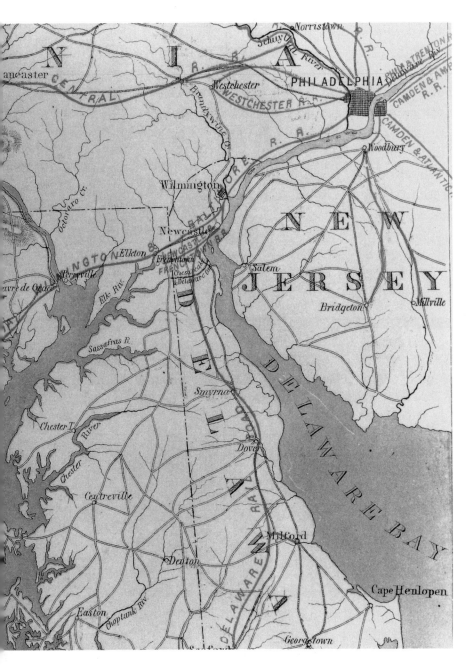

(Prints and Photographs, Maryland Historical Society.)

this invasion of the state. Again, note just what confronted the legislators. Troops were moving toward Baltimore from Philadelphia and from Harrisburg and York. From Gettysburg and Chambersburg troops were moving on Frederick. Other detachments were heading toward the state from Ohio and points west. And troops were already in Annapolis and spreading into Maryland from three sides of Washington.

The House of Delegates refused to approve a request by Baltimore City authorities to reopen the railroads to the North, stating that it simply would be inadvisable. Their poignant response to the Baltimoreans read in part:

> facilities for invasion were offered to the fanatical and excited multitudes of the northern cities . . . whose animosity to Baltimore and Maryland is measured by no standard known to Christian civilization, and who publicly threaten our destruction, without subordination even to the Federal authority. . . . it would hardly be consistent with the commonest prudence to reopen the avenues which would bring them to our very doors.[68]

And so April 1861 drew to a close. For Marylanders, it began in high anxiety over whether the Union would be preserved, and it ended with the beginning of the military occupation of the state by Northern troops and the subjugation of her political will by the force of the federal government.

Four general conclusions can be drawn from the events of April relative to the secession of Maryland:

(1) During the first half of the month, Maryland's reaction to the Lincoln administration was similar to that of the rest of the upper South, and especially Virginia. It strongly opposed coercion of the South, and took a wait-and-see approach toward secession, hoping that some compromise would be reached to save the Union.

(2) With Lincoln's Proclamation of Insurrection and call for troops to suppress the rebellion, Maryland again responded in a manner similar to the upper South by refusing to answer the call and by erupting in opposition to Northern troops passing through the state.

(3) Lincoln and his administration, because of the importance of Washington's security, early on decided that Maryland must be neutralized at all costs and moved aggressively to isolate and then occupy the state as soon as adequate troops were available and plans readied for execution.

(4) The Maryland legislature, knowing that the state was cut off from the South, and knowing that it was powerless to prevent Northern troops from occupying the state and from seizing state and private property and resources, acted accordingly and refused to consider secession.

The events of April just stunned Marylanders—in the magnitude of the response by the Northern states to Lincoln's call for troops, and in the speed in which the response came. As previously noted, in an era when all things moved slowly, the rapidity of the response by the Northern states was astonishing. Again, the chronology of events which overtook Maryland that April:

April 15—Lincoln issued his Proclamation and call for troops;

April 17—Virtually every Northern state answered Lincoln's call enthusiastically, and troops began to move toward Washington (and Maryland);

April 19—Marylanders attempted to stop Northern troops from crossing their state to make war on the South;

April 22—Northern troops took possession of Annapolis,

thereby controlling the state capital and the machinery of the state's administration;

April 24—Northern troops seized and took control of the railroad between Annapolis and Washington and took control of the Chesapeake Bay, thereby isolating Baltimore, and Maryland, from the South;

April 25—Northern troops forced open the railroad to Washington, and a steady flow of troops began to move through the state;

April 26—The legislature convened in Frederick; the federal command ordered their military forces to prevent the state from seceding;

April 27—General Winfield Scott and Secretary of War Simon Cameron distributed their plans for the military occupation of Baltimore and Maryland;

April 28—Maryland was divided into three military departments by federal authorities, and the plan to occupy the state with military force began to be implemented;

April 30—Thousands of Northern troops had massed in cities and towns just north of Maryland and were in the process of entering the state.

For the secessionists of Maryland, the events of April unfolded so rapidly that they were unable to react quickly enough to secure their own destiny. Virginia acted on secession so late, on April 17, after Lincoln's call for troops, and the Northern states responded so quickly and so massively—thousands of troops were in Maryland by April 23—that Maryland was under control before its secessionists could unite and act. Marylanders were acutely aware of the fact that it was their ground, their towns, their homes that would be consumed by a military conflict, and now they found themselves unprepared and unable to stop the invasion of their state. Maryland's Bradley T. Johnson, who would rise to brigadier general in the Confederate army, wrote after the war, "It was too late for Maryland to cut with the Confederacy. There never had been an hour when she could have struck a blow for independence. It was impossible to move before Virginia. Virginia did not move until May 24th, when Maryland was bound hand and foot to the Union by the overwhelming force of the army of occupation."[69]

Virginia did vote to secede on April 17, but an interesting supposition to ponder is this: If Richmond had been cut off from the South as was Baltimore, and if Virginia had been occupied by overwhelming numbers of federal troops as was Maryland, would the Unionist majority in the Virginia State Convention have voted to secede?

As to the true feelings of Marylanders, Mayor George Brown of Baltimore wrote, "After the President's proclamation was issued, no doubt a large majority of her people sympathized with the South."[70] Scharf wrote of Baltimoreans on that fateful April 19: "The whole population rose as by a single impulse to resist the invasion. There was no question of party or class; all differences, all distinctions, were merged in the common feeling."[71]

The secession movement in Maryland probably would have been successful if Marylanders had been free to choose, because a majority of her people favored the South. An even larger majority opposed the North, Lincoln's policies, and the Republican Party. Bruce Catton felt that Maryland remained in the Union because the secessionist leaders of the state were arrested. Harold Manakee seemed to support Catton, "Many of the secessionist leaders were outstanding men in the state, and their voices were heard. Many of the Unionists were small farmers, tradesmen and laborers. Without influential leadership, their voices were lost."[72]

Conversely, why did the secession movement fail in Mary-

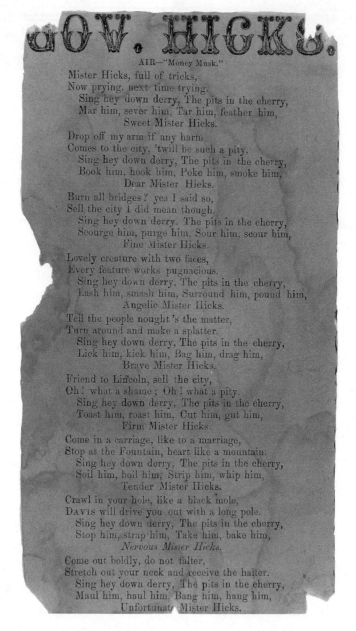

GOV. HICKS.

AIR—"Money Musk."

Mister Hicks, full of tricks,
Now prying, next time trying.
    Sing hey down derry, The pits in the cherry,
    Mar him, sever him, Tar him, feather him,
        Sweet Mister Hicks.

Drop off my arm if any harm
Comes to the city, 'twill be such a pity.
    Sing hey down derry, The pits in the cherry,
    Book him, hook him, Poke him, smoke him,
        Dear Mister Hicks.

Burn all bridges? yes I said so,
Sell the city I did mean though.
    Sing hey down derry, The pits in the cherry,
    Scourge him, purge him, Sour him, scour him,
        Fine Mister Hicks.

Lovely creature with two faces,
Every feature works pugnacious.
    Sing hey down derry, The pits in the cherry,
    Lash him, smash him, Surround him, pound him,
        Angelic Mister Hicks.

Tell the people nought's the matter,
Turn around and make a splatter.
    Sing hey down derry, The pits in the cherry,
    Lick him, kick him, Bag him, drag him,
        Brave Mister Hicks.

Friend to Lincoln, sell the city,
Oh! what a shame; Oh! what a pity.
    Sing hey down derry, The pits in the cherry,
    Toast him, roast him, Cut him, gut him,
        Firm Mister Hicks.

Come in a carriage, like to a marriage,
Stop at the Fountain, heart like a mountain.
    Sing hey down derry, The pits in the cherry,
    Soil him, boil him, Strip him, whip him,
        Tender Mister Hicks.

Crawl in your hole, like a black mole,
DAVIS will drive you out with a long pole.
    Sing hey down derry, The pits in the cherry,
    Stop him, strap him, Take him, bake him,
        Nervous Mister Hicks.

Come out boldly, do not falter,
Stretch out your neck and receive the halter.
    Sing hey down derry, The pits in the cherry,
    Maul him, haul him, Bang him, hang him,
        Unfortunate Mister Hicks.

The song, "Governor Hicks," expressed Marylanders' disdain for their governor. Many secessionists bitterly accused Hicks of selling out the state and Baltimore to the administration in Washington. (Courtesy, Frederick D. Shroyer.)

land? William C. Wright summed it up this way: "When the legislature was finally called into special session, the Union Army was moving across Maryland and it was too late. . . . The force of the federal government and the fact that large numbers of federal troops poured across the state made it impossible for Maryland's secession sympathizers to unite and repel the troops."[73] And Mayor Brown concluded with this bit of logic: ". . . it was clear to all who had not lost their reason that Maryland, which lay open from the North by both land and sea, would be kept in the Union for the sake of the national capital, even if it required the united power of the nation to accomplish the object."[74]

Could the Maryland legislature have voted to secede in the spring of 1861? At least two noted Maryland historians of the era did not think so. "The occupation of the soil of Maryland, and the seizure of railroads and other works of internal improvement partially or wholly owned by the state were denounced as an outrage upon the honor of the state," wrote George Radcliffe. "The resolutions also provided for the appointment of . . . commissioners to communicate in person with Lincoln, and to protest against the treatment of Maryland as a "conquered province." The resolutions were agreed to by both houses without a dissenting vote.[75] Scharf, in reviewing the work of the legislature, eloquently concluded:

> On the appointed day the legislature assembled at Frederick and entered upon the discharge of its duties with earnestness and spirit. Fully impressed with the gravity of the situation, thoroughly comprehending the nature of the crisis, and the perilous situation of our own state, resolutely bent upon vindicating the rights of the South, and protecting the honor and interests of Maryland. . . . During its brief session it passed several useful laws, and kept faithful watch and ward over the interests and honor of Maryland. More than this it could not

do. It was powerless to relieve the state of the presence of strange troops within her borders, and unable to devise any sufficient measures for her protection against the dangers which threatened her. But it honestly exposed the lawless and aggressive character of the policy of which she was victim, it sternly protested against the unconstitutional acts of the administration and its agents, and it showed itself ready, at all times, to discharge, fairly and courageously, the duties which the laws and the Constitution of Maryland devolved upon her representatives.[76]

During those crucial days of April 1861, Lincoln and his commanders determined that their fundamental mission was to preserve the nation. In order to accomplish this, they had to secure the nation's capital at Washington. They could not permit Washington to be surrounded by hostile territory on all sides, and they had to control the railroads that connected the capital to the North and West. Convinced by the Northern press and by key members of his cabinet that Maryland would secede, Lincoln ordered the military to treat Maryland as if she had seceded. In fact, in early March Seward, again the leader of the moderate Republicans, had warned Lincoln that Maryland would secede if he delivered a strongly worded inaugural address. "A tone of desperate earnestness marked the letter Seward sent to the president-elect. He warned bluntly that the original draft would, if delivered, drive Maryland and Virginia out of the Union."[77]

Thus was Maryland neutralized. While other states of the South seceded peacefully and of their own free will, Maryland could not. In the final analysis, Maryland was forced to stay in the Union.

5

The End

That evening old Jack had us out on review,
When a glance down the line showed us all something new—
Eighty-seven young boys from old Baltimore,
Who had run the blockade and that day joined the corps,
Their clothes were resplendent, all new, spick and span
Twas plain that a tailor had measured each man.
When we learned who they were what a shout we did raise!
How we cheered our new allies, the "Baltimore Grays!"

J. D. M'Cabe, Jr.[1]

The end for the secession movement in Maryland, at least the *de jure* end, came on November 6, 1861, with the Union Party's overwhelming victory in the state legislative contests and the election of their candidate, Augustus W. Bradford, as governor.

The election destroyed secessionist hopes of taking Maryland into the Confederacy, and many Marylanders who sympathized with the South fled across the Potomac to join fellow citizens who had already been recruited to Confederate arms by a station set up in Baltimore. Following the election, federal authorities with state cooperation "promptly suppressed all signs of secession sympathy of an active nature. . . . Maryland became in fact as well as in name a loyal state."[2]

Bradford, until 1861 a relatively little known politician, was an unconditional Unionist and therefore received the support of the Lincoln administration, as did his Union Party. Marylanders referred to him as the War Governor. Indeed, he scored an impressive victory—the margins of which were so skewed that many question their authenticity. Bradford won with 57,500 votes to his opponent's 26,000, and his party won sixty-eight seats in the House of Delegates to only six for the opposition. Secessionists and others opposed to Lincoln naturally cried foul. The *Baltimore South* gave its "Union friends . . . great credit for the moderation exercised as there was no earthly reason, beyond the expense of ticket printing, why the majority (in the City of Baltimore) should not have been 40,000 instead of 14,000." The journal had been "reliably informed that the Federal troops from every section of the country kindly aided their Union friends here, and deposited their ballots in as many wards and precincts as suited their convenience."[3] This wry report from a secessionist newspaper should be read for what it is, but Clark makes the compelling point that, "The size of the majority made no difference for the Lincoln administration could have made it what it chose by applying the test oath more strictly, and by arresting State Rights men." He characterized Bradford's election as "perhaps the least satisfactory feature of his entire career" and doubted that he was responsible for the military pressure brought to bear on his behalf. On the other hand, "it is certain that he had knowledge of the way in which his success was brought about. . . . a large proportion of his vote was secured by intimidation, the illegal voting of soldiers, and the unlawful use of soldiery.[4]

Bradford did appear to have been elected by fraudulent means, and some question, given the results, why an election was held at all. It was held, of course, because the Lincoln administration badly wanted the country, and the European governments closely watching developments across the Atlantic, to believe that, constitutionally speaking, things were still working normally and that most Americans supported the administration. Once Lincoln and the War Department determined that Maryland had to be neutralized, they were forced to implement drastic policies. May 1861 saw the completion of the military occupation of the state. Newspapers in Maryland and the North constantly, and rather accurately, reported on troop movements and public opinion. We will continue to use the *Baltimore Sun* and the *New York Times* as our two representative newspapers.

April had ended with the War Department's plan for the occupation of Baltimore in place. Winfield Scott required control of Maryland's railroads and highways and anxiously awaited news from the field. His commanders had some very real problems. First, they did not have enough equipment to outfit the troops flooding in upon them as the North answered Lincoln's call—there were too few tents, kitchen supplies and eating utensils, not even enough rifles. Secondly, the recruits were raw and needed training before they could march, shoot, and do the work of soldiering.

On May 1, General Patterson in Philadelphia informed the War Department that he was positioning his troops for a move on Baltimore and that he expected the railroads to be secured and repaired in a few days.

> I have . . . posted unequipped regiments in camps of instruction at points from which they can be easily withdrawn and distributed. . . . At York, 6 regiments; Chambersburg, 2; Lancaster, 6; Harrisburg, number unknown, but probably 6; and in this vicinity, 6. . . . I have directed these commands to be drilled and made efficient, and by the time they are equipped, I hope to be able to move on Baltimore with an effective force of six thousand men via York and six thousand via Havre de Grace, and have sufficient to guard the road as

they advance. . . . The railroad companies here, and also via York to Baltimore, are now ready to repair their roads, but the troops cannot advance. As soon as the men are equipped they will be thrown to the front, and in a few days the lines will be in working order.[5]

That same day Patterson told Secretary of War Cameron, "Just now the North seems to be spoiling for a fight with Baltimore, and if there is to be one, I repeat the sooner [it] comes off the better."[6]

The Northern press still howled for revenge on Baltimore and for the subjugation of Maryland. And they continued to report on preparations to accomplish this end. The *New York Times* on May 1 headlined: "The Continuous Tide of Money and Men from the North." Newspapers in Maryland repeated this news and also reported on troop movements just north of the border. Baltimore was in a state of shock with business and commerce at a virtual standstill. According to the *Baltimore Sun,* "The late excitement in the city has almost entirely subsided. . . . Everything is dull and the wharves present an almost desolate prospect. . . . Yesterday, at Pratt Street wharf, usually crowded with vessels, there were two small sloops."[7]

May 1 was also the day Secretary of the Navy Gideon Wells established the "Potomac Flotilla," a new naval organization, to patrol the Potomac River and the Chesapeake Bay. This was critically important, for it not only secured the Potomac River, the only waterway to Washington for transporting troops and supplies, but permanently cut off Maryland from Virginia and the Confederacy. Thus, Maryland was isolated from the South—from whence men, arms, and supplies were to have been forthcoming for her defense.

As an aside the *New York Times* on May 2 suggested employing the same "experiment so successfully tried in Maryland" on Virginia—"the presence of an armed force sufficient to put down the mob, now as rampant in the former State as it was a few days ago in the latter." "Reason is returning to Maryland," the *Times* continued, "simply by a demonstration of force." Secession was the result of the mob, the paper argued. "The army stationed at Washington should immediately advance South to act as a local police. The mob at Richmond would prove to be as cowardly and contemptible as at Baltimore."

But the *Baltimore Sun* of the same day reflected a much different sentiment—apprehension at the large numbers of Northern troops marching on Maryland and the matter of just what they intended to do once they arrived. Marylanders were in a state of great anxiety as they read of troop buildups just north of the border and as they began to see their towns and cities occupied by Northern troops. The *Sun* fanned these anxieties, reprinting from the *New York Herald* of May 1:

Baltimore is to be completely filled with troops, and Maryland is to be compelled to act like a State still in the Union. All the information which reached us up to a late hour last night plainly indicated that this is the policy of the government at Washington. . . . The greatest activity prevails in South Pennsylvania, seventeen thousand troops being in the field at the present time. At Camp Scott, York Pennsylvania there are 6,000 men; at Camp Siffler, near Chambersburg, 2,600; at Camp Curtin, near Harrisburg, 4,000; two regiments from Ohio are quartered near Lancaster; and 1,200 U.S. regulars at Carlisle. Scattered at different points between Philadelphia, Elkton and Perryville, there are 6,000 more. Three thousand New Jersey troops are to march from Trenton to-day . . . their destination being undoubtedly for Baltimore.[8]

Indeed, as Marylanders saw it, they were about to be invaded by hordes from the North, and the state's defenses were simply incapable of dealing with the overwhelming numbers at the gates, even if the authorities ordered them to resist. This fact of course was not lost on Maryland's secessionists and certainly not on the governor or members of the legislature. To make matters worse, Virginia was in a state of utter turmoil in its all-out effort to organize forces for its own defense and was thus unable to offer any substantive support to Maryland.

That was the case for the South in general, as both cotton states and the Upper South scurried about in frantic preparation for war. It should be no surprise, then, that General Scott could report to Lincoln, "another change of temper on the part of Maryland in favor of the Union." This change of temper certainly was influenced by the circumstances in which Marylanders found themselves—cut off from the South and in the process of being invaded by thousands of Northern troops. It can well be argued that this "change of temper" was not a sudden surge of Union sentiment but an urge for self preservation. The situation had tilted in favor of the Lincoln administration. With new troops arriving in Washington daily, with the railway and telegraph through Maryland now at least partially opened, and with reports of troops massing just north of the Maryland border, the confidence of the War Department rose hourly. On May 3, Scott ordered General Butler to occupy Relay, Maryland, a key junction on the Baltimore and Ohio Railroad, where trains from the north and from the west could be controlled. At the same time, Secretary of War Cameron informed Philadelphia authorities that the jig was up for Maryland—they would submit to federal domination or else.

> In my judgement the sooner the line via Annapolis is perfected the better. It will have a good effect in bringing our Maryland friends to terms. The administration cannot afford to temporize with Baltimore. They [the people of Baltimore and Maryland at large] must agree to restore the property they have destroyed, and make reparation for damages, before we can open communication by their city. They must also agree

that the Federal Government shall have the absolute right to move troops through their city, or quarter them in it or any part of the State of Maryland. Northern sentiment on this question is overwhelming and just in every respect.

In fact discussions had taken place with the authorities in Baltimore, and Cameron reported, "In a very few days Baltimore will be at work reconstructing the works destroyed by authority under color of mob violence." And indeed, Baltimore began to surrender on this day when a report reached the War Department stating, "The authorities of Baltimore, having proclaimed that the transit shall be open for troops to this place, have requested that the first body that comes through shall be headed by regulars."[9]

Faced with hopeless odds against their beloved city, Baltimore secessionists indeed had few choices. They were isolated from the South by Butler's troops in Annapolis and the Potomac Flotilla. Northern troops were moving toward them from Philadelphia, Harrisburg, Gettysburg, Chambersburg, and points west. Baltimoreans had food and supplies to sustain the city for only a few days and no real means to defend themselves. Their militia was ill-trained and even more ill-equipped for any large-scale fighting. Three articles from the *Sun* of May 3 aptly illustrate. The first, "The Blockade of Virginia Ports," reported:

The steamers Adelaide . . . and Louisiana . . . of the Bay Line bound to Norfolk returned to this port yesterday. The Adelaide, which left here on Tuesday, proceeded as far as Old Point Comfort, where Capt. Cannon was notified by Commander Pendergast, of the blockading fleet, that under no circumstances would he be allowed to go to Norfolk. . . . The only ship of war off the Point was the Cumberland, but the number of steamers, tugs, transports and small craft, all mounted with cannon and well-manned, was almost innumerable. They were stopping and overhauling every passing vessel.

The second article, under the headline, "The New Military Departments," described the division of Maryland into three military districts,

> An important order from the War Department—a brief notice of which has been heretofore been made—constitutes three new military departments, the first of which composes the District of Columbia, according to its original boundary, Fort Washington and adjacent country and the State of Maryland as far as Bladensburg inclusive. The second is the department of Annapolis, with headquarters at that city, and including the country for twenty miles on each side of the railroad from Annapolis to Washington, as far as Bladensburg, and the third is the department of Pennsylvania, and includes that State, Delaware and all of Maryland not included in the other two. The same order transfers the Annapolis Naval School to Ft. Adams.

The third article, entitled "Plan of the Campaign," reported on what lay in store for Baltimore:

> A correspondent of the Philadelphia Inquirer writes: By putting together the facts which I have gathered from several officers just from Washington, it becomes quite evident that the War Department has made arrangements for carrying on the war on a scale of magnitude not yet intimated, and with a vigor and determination that must insure success. The first operation of the campaign will be the military occupation of Baltimore, and that part of the Philadelphia, Wilmington and Baltimore railroad between Havre de Grace and Baltimore, the rebuilding of all the bridges between the latter two points, the establishment of another camp at Havre de Grace, and the concentration of an army of fifty thousand men at Washington, of whom due proportion shall be artillery and cavalry. These movements will all be executed by the 10th of May.

This correspondent, as it turned out, had reliable information. Imagine the distress Marylanders felt when confronted by these reports—and imagine the impact on the legislature assembled at Frederick.

On May 4, the military buildup continued with increased momentum. The *Sun* reported from Annapolis:

> There are between 5,000 and 6,000 troops here. . . . seven hundred troops left Annapolis in a steamer bound out last night, with a battery. It is generally understood that they were ordered to land near Baltimore, to co-operate with troops approaching that city from the North. . . . The New Jersey volunteers, in from ten to thirteen schooners, are hourly expected at Annapolis. The facilities for transportation are quite complete between Annapolis and Perryville. The passage is made in three and a half hours. Twelve steamers are employed in the route.

And on this day, the usually moderate *Sun* delivered a stinging editorial on the Lincoln administration's policies toward Maryland,

> . . . it is very certain that such practices prevail as are calculated to embarrass the trade and seriously affect the convenience of the people; and apparently with the connivance, if not the sanction, of the general government. Yet at the same time the most friendly relations are professed towards our city and State. The two things are incompatible and absurd, yet they exist. Of course, no one can be deceived by them. . . . The government is evidently pursuing such a course as is calculated to annoy, injure and impoverish our city; at the same time affects a fair face and says it does not wish to harm us. The government has the sole control of the avenues to the city, and has blockaded our rivers, canals and bay, and has shut up Baltimore from all commerce and trade. . . . The embargo is almost as complete as if Maryland were a seceded State. . . . The last blockade was

declared against Virginia and North Carolina, and is made just as effective against Maryland, but especially against this city.

Of course the Lincoln administration wanted desperately to convince the country (and the world) that they were doing good, but in reality they moved aggressively to subjugate Maryland by military force. Again, it is important to note, as illustrated in chapter 4 and the ongoing discussion here, that from April 15 to November 6 Lincoln and the War Department treated Maryland as if she had seceded.

Next, the moderate Northern press turned on Maryland with a vengence. The *New York Times* of May 4 ran this headline: "Treacherous Action of the Maryland Legislature." Its editorial of the day, entitled "The Relations of Maryland to the Union" launched an attack on the Maryland legislature.

[W]e have never had entire faith in the conversion alleged to have been wrought—almost by miracle—among the Secessionists of Maryland. We attribute, justly, no doubt, very great efficacy to the presence of a superior force on her borders, and to the moral influence of the general uprising in the North, in restoring the reign of reason and moderation. . . . Our worst apprehensions have been confirmed by the extraordinary proceedings in the Maryland Legislature, which we published yesterday. . . . The movement in the Maryland Legislature, is of a piece with all the movements of this diabolical treason from the commencement. . . . No more parleying with traitors!

In their own diabolical verse, they went on to say what must have become obvious to the secessionists of Maryland:

The Maryland Quickstep—The State of Maryland is said now to "keep step to the music of the Union." Her sudden return to the Union column is a marvelous conversion. . . . We don't doubt the sincerity of Baltimore's conversion. She saw "line upon line" of good soldiers coming; and she heard "here a little and there a"—great deal of persuasion; and she has drummed herself into the Union column. Perhaps, after all, the world moves. But how long before Virginia and Jefferson Davis are taught the Maryland quickstep.

Marylanders would continue to take the heat for some time to come. Organized resistance or overt opposition to the federals began to dissipate throughout the state.

On the fifth, Butler notified the War Department that he had occupied Relay House and assured them that with his present force he could "march through Baltimore." He went on to report that "for several days many of the armed secessionists have left for Harper's Ferry or have gone forth plundering the country." In fact, Colonel Isaac Ridgway Trimble knew that the Maryland militia had no chance against the overwhelming numbers of Northern troops descending on the state and on May 6 ordered the local guard units disbanded. Baltimore was now defenseless with federal troops only nine miles from the city. More to the point, they controlled all west- and southbound railway traffic as well as the Chesapeake Bay and the entrance to the Baltimore harbor via troops at Forts McHenry and Carroll. The War Department authorized General Butler to arrest "persons who commit acts of hostility" and to inspect and restrict, if necessary, any and all trains which passed over the lines he controlled.

On May 7 the authorities in Maryland decided to give up and offer no further resistance to the federal military. Mayor Brown consulted with the city council and stated that the people of Maryland had "decided to submit to the Federal Government." The *Baltimore Sun* reported on the special legislative caucus of the day before. Commissioners, sent by the legislature to confer with Lincoln and his cabinet, returned to the legislature and counselled it to submit to the overwhelming force of the federal army. Speaking for the commission, the Hon. R. M. McLane relayed to a joint session of the General Assembly his impression that "it was the intention of the Cabinet to subjugate the seceding States by gradual approaches of troops to sustain the Union men of Virginia and Tennessee especially, and by whose aid the Cabinet expected that the secessionists of those States would be overcome without bloodshed." Maryland and the District of Columbia would be "necessarily occupied to some extent as a rendezvous for troops and a depot for munitions of war." McLane urged all members to "devote themselves exclusively to the preservation of the peace and safety of Maryland in the present crisis . . . because whilst the State is occupied by the federal troops, it would be physically impossible to relieve her from political association with the federal government." In his concluding remarks, McLane strongly rejected the policies of the Lincoln administration. "Honorable and true-hearted men . . . will never consent to maintain the Union by shedding the blood of the Southern people and subjugating the Southern States. Therefore such men can never again support the administration of Mr. Lincoln, which has now abandoned the defensive policy of maintaining the federal capital. . . ." McLane went on to urge Governor Hicks, "to stand by the true interest and true men of the State, leaving to the administration only the ruffian and venal portion of our population." Lincoln and his cabinet had officially notified Maryland authorities that the state would be occupied by the federal military—and McLane, one of Maryland's most respected citizens, wisely urged the legislature to offer no organized resistance.[10]

On May 8, the *New York Times* headlined, "Northern Troops to Go Through Baltimore To-day." The following day, the *Baltimore Sun* reported under "Military Movements in Pennsylvania": "The books show that 163 companies, besides the eight Philadelphia regiments, have been accepted and mustered into service. . . . The entire number is 41,500." Practically all of these troops were put in motion toward Maryland—and these were the forces from just one Northern state. There were indeed hordes of Northerners moving toward Maryland. Organized resistance in Maryland continued to crumble as large numbers of federal troops deployed across the countryside. Northerners began to do some muscle flexing, and Pennsylvania came close to declaring war on Maryland as reported in the *Sun* of May 9.

> The report of the select committee on that portion of the Governor's message relative to the killing of the troops at Baltimore, made this afternoon, recites the facts and demands the punishment of all persons taking part in the murders, the release of all citizens from Pennsylvania unjustly confined at Baltimore, and authorizes the Governor to take such measures as he may deem best to effect these purposes.

Marylanders had few options left. They either submitted to the federals or they headed South to join the Confederacy.

On May 10, the *Baltimore Sun* published one of its last unfettered editorials and certainly one of its most profound. Entitled, "The Practical and the Impractical," it was a summary of why Maryland stayed in the Union. The editorial concluded forcefully:

> There is no doubt, and our experience confirms the belief, that the great majority of our citizens, would to-day, if the independence of the Confederate States, including Virginia, were about to be recognized, vote to unite the State of Maryland and the City of Baltimore with the Southern Nation. We say that this is our firm belief.

On May 13, General Butler, aware that the Maryland militiamen were fleeing Baltimore and feeling more secure about General Patterson's ability to reenforce him, moved his troops into the city. He placed his cannon on Federal Hill and aimed them at prominent points in the city including Baltimoreans' beloved Washington Monument, which he threatened to blow up at the first sign of trouble.

> About sunset May 13, 1861, a train pulled into Camden Station from Relay House. Aboard were Gen. Benj. F. Butler and troops including about 500 men of the 6th Massachusetts Infantry, the regiment stoned less than a month before on Pratt Street. Butler established himself on Federal Hill, fortified the same and sent a note to Major Morris commanding at Fort McHenry. In this note the general advised the major that he had "taken possession of Baltimore" and asked the major to fire upon Monument Square if Butler were attacked during the night.[11]

The next day, Butler proclaimed to the citizens, "A detachment of the forces of the Federal Government under my command have occupied the city of Baltimore for the purpose, among other things, of enforcing respect and obedience to the laws."[12] "Among other things" meant the immediate cessation of any and all acts of support for the South, including the display of the Confederate flag.

Butler and his troops were not welcomed in Baltimore. "The city General Butler occupied on 13 May, . . . did not fill the streets with celebrations and parades but rather with a peculiar silence and reticence." Mayor Brown reacted with contempt and "refused to assist Butler with his official duties." The Baltimore newspapers suddenly fell silent, their accounts of the initial days of occupation "notably bland, merely descriptive."[13] Winfield Scott, however, was not silent. Proclaiming it a "God-send" that Baltimore was occupied without a clash of arms, Scott on May 15 replaced Butler with General George Cadwalader as commander of troops in the city.

Although Butler had angered Scott by moving on Baltimore

without explicit orders, Lincoln within days promoted him to the rank of major general. Baltimore was put under martial law for the remainder of the war. Baltimoreans did not resist but joined many Southerners who would hate the name of Butler for a generation. In Butler's defense, his actions saved the city, and like New Orleans (which Butler also occupied and where he earned the sobriquet "Beast"), Baltimore came through the war relatively unscathed.

On May 14, the *New York Times* trumpeted: "Baltimore Occupied by Federal Troops"; "Martial Law To Be Declared"; "The Troops Encamped on Federal Hill"; "The Direct Route Through Baltimore Open Again." The paper haughtily declared:

> The passage of fourteen hundred U.S. troops through Baltimore . . . constitutes an epoch in the war long to be remembered. It was a peaceful triumph over the secession mob, and furnishes an instructive lesson for the future. The Marylanders are as high spirited as their more Southern brethren, and with far more wealth, and with all the advantages of concentrated force of numbers, we have seen the Secessionists of the State gracefully surrender the control of the greatest city in the South without firing a gun in their defence.

On May 16 the *Baltimore Sun* changed its headline column to read, "Military Movements in Baltimore." On the twentieth, its editorial blasted the North as the War Party, supported the South, and called for a peaceful settlement of the conflict.

Some historians have interpreted Lincoln's policy of moderation—that is, his moderate use of force—toward Maryland in late April and early May as judicious and even benevolent. But the facts suggest that his War Department had no other choice at that time. They did not have enough troops (at least troops trained and equipped for combat), and they did not have means to transport them (at least not through Maryland). Their only option was to bide time. By mid-May they did have enough troops and they had, at least partially, secured the railroads and the waterways so as to be able to move. And move with dispatch they did. Winfleld Scott was a superb military strategist and certainly demonstrated his capabilities during this time.

With the two principal cities of Maryland—Annapolis and Baltimore—under military control, the federal government moved rapidly to consolidate its position. In quick succession Butler ordered the arrest of Ross Winans, noted inventor and a member of the Maryland legislature; Lincoln suspended the writ of habeas corpus throughout the state; military commanders were given authority to arrest Marylanders "under certain circumstances"; Northern troops almost immediately secured and repaired the Northern Central, the Philadelphia, Wilmington and Baltimore, and the B&O railroads, thereby opening several all-rail routes between Washington and the North; and Northern troops, with nothing to stop them, marched into Maryland by the thousands. Matthew Page Andrews concluded:

> Butler proved to be no respecter of personal or state rights. For Constitutional guarantees he cared nothing at all. Having established martial law, he asserted he had "captured" the city, and was made a major general in recognition of the achievement. After May 21st the federal government did not consider that there was further need to send troops around the city; for Maryland was regarded as being safely under military domination.[14]

Meanwhile, in Frederick, with their state fast being occupied by Northern troops, Maryland legislators continued to meet. The General Assembly had gone on record advocating recognition of the Southern Confederacy, but now in early May, long and for the most part unproductive debate attempted to frame the issue and decide on a course of action. With frayed nerves and flared tempers, legislators argued with one another, the House of Delegates fought with the Senate, and everyone belabored the governor. Rumors of plots against Hicks's life abounded. The legislature approved the actions of Virginia, went out of its way to maintain cordial relations with that state, and opposed the Lincoln administration in every way.

On May 9, the House of Delegates' Committee on Federal Relations finally came forward with its report. The resolutions strongly protested the policy of coercion adopted by the federal government and condemned military occupation as a "flagrant violation of the Constitution." The committee also asked that the Southern Confederacy be recognized by the United States. Most importantly for Maryland, the report declared that "under existing conditions it is not expedient to call a sovereign convention of the state at this time."[15] The lower house adopted the resolutions by a vote of forty-three to thirteen, the senate by eleven to three. Strongly pro-Southern as this "Rebel Legislature" was, it had little choice but reject an immediate call for secession. "The rapid course of events was constantly rendering more imperative either a policy of inaction, or an endorsement of the federal administration. The latter the legislature most assuredly would not give."[16]

To summarize, Marylanders in mid-May faced the following: Butler was in possession of Baltimore and the Relay House and thereby in control of virtually all railroad activity in the state. The Potomac Flotilla patrolled the Potomac River and Chesapeake Bay without opposition—Virginia and the Confederacy had no navy. Northern troops were marching across Maryland's northern border, and some had started toward Frederick, where the legislature was in session. Annapolis was occupied by Northern troops who thereby controlled the state's administrative machinery. Washington had been reenforced by thousands of Northern troops, who were taking up positions in

Maryland around the District. The Northern press was unrelenting in its call for revenge on Baltimore and for the subjugation of Maryland. And the largely pro-Southern Maryland militia had been disbanded. Given this state of the state, it was remarkable that the legislature took such a strong and determined anti-Lincoln stand. But Lincoln and his administration would not forget the legislators' defiance, as subsequent events in the summer and fall of 1861 would attest.

Unquestionably, the aggressive actions of the federal military in Maryland during late April and early May had a profound impact on the members of the legislature. The occupation of the state by the federal military simply overawed the pro-southern majority while at the same time it encouraged and emboldened the Unionist minority. Resolutions—words of condemnation—were the order of the day, whereas action—a vote on secession—was not.

In the final analysis then, the legislature simply could not have passed an ordinance of secession in the presence of federal troops. This would have precipitated an instant clash between the Northern troops in Maryland (who, it will be remembered, were under orders "to bomb their cities" in the event of secession) and the pro-Southern Maryland militia and other armed citizens. Everyone knew that the Maryland guard had no chance against such large numbers. Equally important, at this crucial moment Maryland had no unimpeded physical connection with the South. There was no means of supplying arms, reenforcements, indeed food or other essential supplies. She was hopelessly isolated. Scharf wrote after the war:

> These facts stared the Legislature in the face, and they acted in accordance with their duty, and the weighty trust reposed in them, in resisting the mad unreasoning clamors of those who wished to precipitate a conflict. Whatever may have been their personal views of the justice of the war that was

being waged, their first duty was to save the lives and property of Maryland; and they performed that duty firmly and well, as all men now cheerfully admit.[17]

The legislature, under the circumstances, did the only thing it could do by protesting the actions of the Lincoln administration and offering support and encouragment to the Southern Confederacy. It passed resolutions again and again announcing its desire to recognize the Southern government. Lincoln and Jefferson Davis both knew of the legislature's inclination to place Maryland in direct alliance with the Confederacy, and Lincoln was ready by force of arms to check any such steps the General Assembly might take. The legislature knew as much and condemned federal policy in strong language. "There can be no doubt that a majority of the members of the Maryland Legislature desired to see that body take a more advanced position of friendliness to the Confederacy than was really done."[18] The General Assembly adjourned on May 14. On his way home Delegate Ross Winans was arrested by federal troops. Since martial law had not been declared and since Maryland had not seceded, his arrest and imprisonment without a warrant or a charge, was extraordinary.

Charles B. Clark affixed the formal date of the end of the secession movement in Maryland as November 6, 1861, the date the Unconditional Unionists gained control of the state's political apparatus. But it can be argued that the de facto or real date was May 28, 1861.

By late May the federal army was daily increasing its presence in Maryland. At 2 A.M. on the morning of May 25, troops of the 1st Regiment Pennsylvania Volunteers surrounded the home of John Merryman, a Baltimore County farmer and leader of a local

*Roger Brooke Taney, Chief Justice of the Supreme Court in 1861 and a Mary-
lander, challenged Lincoln's use of federal troops in arresting Maryland citizens without charge and called on the president to abide by the Constitution.
After the war, he was roundly applauded for his defense of the law. (Library
of Congress.)*

militia unit known for its pro-Southern stance. They arrested Merryman without a warrant or charge and took him to Fort McHenry. This was the second arbitrary arrest of a prominent Marylander by military authority (Ross Winans was the first), and it set the stage for the famous confrontation between the executive and the judicial branches of the United States government.

The venerable Chief Justice of the Supreme Court, Roger B. Taney, a Marylander, realized the significance of what was happening and personally issued a writ of habeas corpus instructing the federal commander of Fort McHenry to bring Merryman to his court for proper treatment under civilian law. Butler's replacement, General George Cadwalader, refused, stating that by authority of the president he was suspending the writ and would therefore not obey the summons of the highest court in the land. Backed by troops, Cadwalader had the power to resist the orders of the court. Taney became enraged and challenged the authority of the president of the United States to suspend basic constitutional rights.

I ordered the attachment of yesterday because upon the face of the return the detention of the prisoner was unlawful upon two grounds:

1. The President, under the Constitution and laws of the United States, cannot suspend the privilege of the writ of habeas corpus, nor authorize any military officer to do so.

2. A military officer has no right to arrest and detain a person not subject to the rules and articles of war for an offense against the laws of the United States, except in aid of the judicial authority and subject to its control; and if the party is arrested by the military, it is the duty of the officer to deliver him over immediately to the civil authority, to be dealt with according to law.

Thus, Chief Justice Taney called on the president to abide by the Constitution of the United States. Some have argued that Lincoln had no choice, that the precarious situation of the Union took precedence over the Constitution. This produced an interesting debate.

Legal purists of the day remembered Taney for condemning, in the face of military force, the usurpation of the law by what he and they considered to be an overzealous executive. He was roundly applauded for upholding the heritage of English liberty. On leaving the court, the Chief Justice was reported to have told Baltimore's mayor: "Mr. Brown, I am an old man, a very old man; but perhaps I was preserved for this occasion." The Merryman case was not only a direct and ominous clash between the president of the United States and the Chief Justice of the Supreme Court, it was made a test between that which personified the rule of law on one side and the sudden and unlimited development of military force on the other.[19]

The Merryman case has been studied by legal scholars and historians, and it is not within the scope of this work to make any comments relative to jurisprudence.[20] However, it is important to comment on the Merryman case and its impact on the secessionists of Maryland. As demonstrated in chapter 2, most Marylanders supported either the extremist Southern party (those who voted for Breckinridge) or the moderate Southern party (those who voted for Bell). As they had watched Northern troops occupy their cities and towns, they now watched the arbitrary arrest of a prominent citizen, who was forceably removed from his home in the middle of the night. Merryman was a reasonably well-to-do and well-connected farmer, and his arrest captured the attention of all Marylanders. If he could be arrested and imprisoned without charge, then what of the Constitution, the Bill of Rights, and the history of a government ruled by laws? Would federal military forces be allowed to

*Ross Winans, staunchly pro-South-
ern member of the General
Assembly and a highly successful
businessman and inventor, was
the first Marylander to be arbitrarily arrested by federal military
authorities. (Courtesy Daniel D.
Hartzler.)*

forceably capture and imprison citizens at their discretion? One
can see why the state, and indeed the nation, focused on Taney's
courtroom in Baltimore on that late spring day. Bruce Catton
concluded:

> It is presisely that sort of thing that the Constitution was set
> up to prevent. Clause 2, Section 9, Article 1, guarantees every
> citizen the protection of the writ of habeas corpus, under
> which a court can compel the authorities to either release a
> man who has been arrested or to file formal charges against
> him in the regular way and make them stick in the ordinary
> courts of law. The Constitution does say that this writ may
> not be suspended except in case of insurrection or invasion.
> It does not say who is authorized to suspend it in such cases.
> Lincoln simply went ahead on the theory that the president
> did. He came under wide criticism for this and to this day the
> argument still rages. But he succeeded in neutralizing the
> opposition from secessionist forces.[21]

For Marylanders, especially the secessionists, it did neutralize their opposition. For it was at their homes that Butler aimed his guns and it was in their front yards that federal troops congregated. Thus, it can be argued that May 28 was the date on which Maryland's secession movement truly ended. After the war the Supreme Court upheld Taney's courageous decision. "Martial rule can never exist where the courts are open, and in the proper and unobstructed exercise of their jurisdiction."[22] Maryland secessionists now recognized that the game was up and that open and direct opposition to federal authorities was useless. Some continued to resist by sending supplies and weapons south. Others made plans to escape to Virginia to serve the Confederacy. Some found ways to oppose the federals covertly, and still others, for business reasons or just personal gain, became conditional Unionists. A discussion of this latter group is contained in chapter 7.

By the end of May, Governor Hicks, with federal regiments nearly in control of the state, took some bold steps to align himself with the Lincoln administration. On May 30, he ordered all state arms to be seized and turned over to federal authorities. As previously noted, the Maryland militia was predominantly pro-Southern and Hicks, knowing who had won the game in Maryland, moved to demonstrate his commitment to the national government. Of course, his decision outraged the pro-Southern members of the legislature, and when they reconvened on June 4, the Senate immediately asked Hicks to explain his actions, specifically why he had surrendered the state's arms. Hicks's reply did not satisfy the legislature, and they passed a resolution, twelve to four, stating that he had exceeded his authority and calling him a "military despot." Their long-held belief that Hicks was in collaboration with the Lincoln administration now confirmed, the House of Delegates also came to an open breach with the governor. Thus, the two branches of the state government reached a complete impasse. For the remainder of their session, the Rebel Legislature had virtually nothing to do with the turncoat governor, and whenever possible Hicks ignored the legislature. The General Assembly became "more marked in its hostility" toward the United States Government and more openly supportive of the Confederacy. It requested its U.S. Senators, Pearce and Kennedy, "to vote for the recognition of the Confederacy by the United States Government, and to present to the United States Senate for record the solemn protest of the Legislature of Maryland 'against the manifold usurpations and oppressions of the Federal Government.'"[23]

In as much as federal regiments by this time had firm control of the state, one can speculate about why the administration tolerated such defiance. The answer probably is that Lincoln had many more pressing issues to deal with—the movement of Southern troops toward Washington, for example—and hopelessly isolated in Frederick, the "Rebel Legislature" was not going anywhere. In time, the administration would turn its attention back to that body.

June was noteworthy for several other events. First, it was the beginning of formal military operations in the state. On the eighth, an expedition got underway when the War Department ordered Colonel Charles P. Stone of the 14th U. S. Infantry to "march to Edwards Ferry, which you will seize and hold, and, if practical, cross the river and continue on to Leesburg. Intercept supplies sent from Baltimore to Virginia."[24] This was a movement on Rockville, to secure Maryland west and north of Washington, including the ground on the Maryland side of the Potomac upriver toward Harper's Ferry. Cumberland was occupied by Indiana troops on the tenth.

On June 9, with the War Department's approval, Hicks asked General Patterson to occupy Frederick, to guard it against an attack "by rebels at Harper's Ferry." But the rebels at Harper's

Ferry had their hands full trying to organize and equip themselves and, with Union forces moving on them from two directions, were in no position to attack anyone. Of course, everyone recognized that Frederick was the town where the legislature was meeting and thereby the temporary seat of the state government. On the tenth, Patterson replied that he would do it "so soon as I can extend it consistently with the safety of other important interests." A mere six weeks after he had told Lincoln not to send troops to Maryland, the governor was requesting the War Dapartment to occupy the temporary seat of government in the state. Obviously, Hicks wanted federal troops to help him control the legislature.

In Baltimore on June 13 an election was held for the special session of Congress called by Lincoln in his proclamation of April 15. Attention focussed on the contest in the Fourth Congressional District where another former Know-Nothing, Henry Winter Davis, was running as an Unconditional Unionist. Davis, although a politician of great oratorical skill, was truly dispised in the state. At the time, he held the distinction of being the only member of Congress from Maryland to ever have been formally censured by the state legislature, that for his support of a Republican, William Pennington, for Speaker of the House of Representatives. There was great concern that Davis would find a way to use the military to get elected. In fact, he did try to use the army: he reported to Washington that Union men were being driven from the polls and that more troops were needed for their protection (and so that they could vote for him). In the election he was defeated by Henry May, an independent, by a wide margin. The defeat of Davis, an ardent supporter of the Lincoln administration, was not lost on the federal command. In the next election, the gubernatorial election of November 1861, the federal military took an active role to ensure the proper result.

The final noteworthy event of June was the arrest of Marshal George P. Kane, Chief of Police in the City of Baltimore. Kane, accused of a variety of pro-Southern activities, was arrested and imprisoned under the orders of General Nathaniel Preston Banks, who had replaced Cadwalader. Banks placed Baltimore lawyer John R. Kenly, lately colonel of the 1st Maryland Volunteer Regiment, in charge of the city's police. Kenly went to the board of police commissioners, the duly elected civilian authority over the police, and informed them that he had been appointed provost-marshal and that their authority had been superseded. The board and Mayor Brown protested this direct seizure of civilian authority to no avail. The federal military had now declared, for all intents and purposes, martial law and assumed complete control of the city. On July 1, Banks, commanding the Department of Annapolis which included Baltimore, arrested all of the police commissioners and read another proclamation to the citizens of Baltimore:

> In pursuance of orders issued from the Headquarters of the Army at Washington for the preservation of the public peace in this department I have arrested and do now detain in custody of the United States the members of the late board of police, Messrs. Charles Howard, William H. Gatchell, Charles D. Hinks and John W. Davis. They refused to recognize the force necessarily appointed. . . .

> Whenever a loyal citizen can be nominated to the office of marshal who will execute the police laws impartially and in good faith to the United States the military force will be withdrawn at once from the central parts of the municipality.[25]

This completed the military occupation of Baltimore. The Northern press, its revenge exacted, was finally appeased.

The legislature ended the month strongly protesting these illegal actions, but again it was powerless to do anything more.

> Be it resolved, that the Senate and House of Delegates of
> Maryland, in the name of and behalf of the good people of the
> State, do accordingly register this their earnest and unqualified
> protest against the oppression and tyrannical assertion and
> exercise of military jurisdiction, within the limits of Maryland,
> over the persons and property of her citizens, by the govern-
> ment of the United States, and do solemnly declare the same to
> be subversive of the most sacred guarantee of the Constitution,
> and in flagrant violation of the fundamental and most cher-
> ished principle of American free government.[26]

Scharf wrote:

> Thus did the Legislature of the State of Maryland remonstrate
> against the indefensible conduct of the United States Gov-
> ernment. It displayed a spirit of heroism worthy of her
> liberty-loving people. Sitting in a city surrounded, occupied,
> and threatened on all sides by Federal bayonets . . . its calm,
> dignified voice of protest rose like the utterances of Senates
> and Consuls of classic days, and as worthy as they to be
> recorded in history.[27]

Scharf's sentiments may be true, but these resolutions simply
irritated the Lincoln administration further and its patience
with the Rebel Legislature wore increasingly thin.

The summer of 1861 was a bitter one for many Marylanders.
The federal army proceeded with its occupation of the state,
seizing property and arresting citizens at will. Fighting, to various degrees, broke out all over the area. The administration, now
emboldened by its hold on Maryland, moved to consolidate its
grip on her citizens. These events had a profound impact on the
state's waning secession movement.

By late June the federal army had occupied Annapolis, Baltimore, Cumberland, Havre de Grace, Perryville, and assorted
small towns and villages. Pickets were posted around the en-

campments, and small skirmishes occurred periodically. Confederate and Union pickets exchanged shots up and down the Potomac River. A Confederate force burned the railroad bridge over New Creek and threatened Cumberland, sending the city into near panic. Union soldiers were killed at Sandy Hook (near Harper's Ferry) by Confederates firing from the Virginia shore. At Great Falls, just above Washington, a day-long skirmish left two more Union dead. On September 9, Union forces moved out of Bladensburg to occupy Southern Maryland. By the end of September, federal military authorities controlled virtually all police forces, railroads, and major highways in the state.

> Throughout the state railroad bridges and canal locks were under permanent Union guard. Gunboats prowled the Chesapeake Bay. Every bridge and ford across the Potomac River—almost all of the Maryland shore, in fact—was constantly watched. Pickets patrolled vital turnpike points. The huge concentration of troops in Washington spilled over the District of Columbia line into many camps and forts in Prince George's and Montgomery counties. . . . Camp Parole, a large installation for training and for prisoner-of-war exchange, was built west of Annapolis. The grounds of St. John's College and of the Naval School . . . served as hospitals. . . . Strong detachments of soldiers were quartered throughout Southern Maryland and the Eastern Shore. Others were stationed at Frederick, Hagerstown, Clarysville, and Cumberland, where many large buildings of a public nature were commandeered for use as barracks, headquarters, hospitals or supply depots. . . . The list is not exhaustive.[28]

Although Lincoln had called for 75,000 volunteers on April 15, the War Department called for greater numbers throughout the summer of 1861. By fall, those numbers in and around Maryland were simply staggering. Here is the official report of the War Department.

By the 15th of October the number of troops in and about Washington, inclusive of the garrison of the city of Alexandria, the city guard, and the forces on the Maryland shore of the Potomac below Washington, and as far as Cumberland above, the troops under the command of General Dix at Baltimore and its dependencies, were as follows:

Total present for duty 133,201
Total sick 9,290
Total in confinement 1,156

Aggregate present 143,647
Aggregate absent 8,404

Grand Aggregate . . . . . . 152,051[29]

Given this astounding situation, the secessionists of Maryland for the most part either went South to join the Confederacy or went underground to do what they could to oppose the federals.

In spite of the large numbers of Union soldiers guarding important points throughout the state, the Eastern Shore and Southern Maryland never were completely under federal control. Confederate sympathizers in those areas set up definite lines of communication between North and South. Almost routinely swift bay craft on the Chesapeake and small rowboats on the Potomac ran the blockade of Union patrol vessels. . . . Shipments of small, but important, supplies, such as drugs, medicines and percussion caps, reached Confederate hands. . . . Some Maryland Confederates are known to have visited their homes while on leave.

"Unfortunately the stories of most such adventures have been lost to history," wrote Harold Manakee. "Even after the war accounts of them were not written for fear of punishment. Today they live principally as romantic family legends, but they are numerous."[30]

Meanwhile, the federal command moved systematically to consolidate its power and to eliminate its opponents. After the arrests of Marshal Kane and the police commissioners of Baltimore, even some of Lincoln's supporters became nervous about what appeared to be an abuse of power on the part of the chief executive and the federal military. On July 24, the House of Representatives, controlled by the Republicans, sent Lincoln the following resolution: "That the President be requested immediately to communicate to this House if in his judgment not incompatible with the public interest the grounds, reason and evidence upon which the police commissioners of Baltimore were arrested and are now detained as prisoners at Fort McHenry." In a classic example of tongue-in-cheek, Lincoln replied:

> In answer to the resolution of the House of Representatives of the 24th instant asking grounds, reason and evidence upon which the police commissioners of Baltimore were arrested and are now detained as prisoners at Fort McHenry I have to state that it is judged to be incompatible with the public interest at this time to furnish the information called for by the resolution.[31]

Lincoln may have had some fun drafting the reply, but indeed what concerned the Congress was a kind of arbitrary and unwarranted use of power that had inspired American revolutionaries in 1776. Thus, from friend and foe alike, concerns were raised as to the limits of federal power. The scene became more alarming a few weeks later when General Scott directed Colonel Martin Burke, commander of Fort Hamilton, New York, where the political prisoners were being held, "Should the writ of habeas corpus come for the production in court of any of your political prisoners you will respond thereto that you deeply regret that pending existing political troubles you cannot comply with the requisition of the honorable judge." And a few days later he commanded, "You will resist any attempt to take your person on a writ of attachment."[32]

It appeared that the federal military, at the direction of the president, was setting itself above the courts and laws of the land, indeed, a most remarkable circumstance. For Marylanders, that was particularly ominous. For here was a state that had not formally seceded, where martial law had *not* been formally declared, yet where the federal military arrested and imprisoned citizens without charge and seized private property at will.

On August 20, the War Department instructed General John A. Dix, Banks's replacement in command at Baltimore,

> Before many days some place will be designated where prisoners of this description can be sent for safe-keeping until everything is settled. When there is good reason to suppose that persons are giving aid and comfort to the enemy they should be arrested even when there is a want of positive proof of their guilt.[33]

The phrases "good reasons to suppose" and "want of positive proof" meant that anyone could be suspect and thereby arrested. Indeed, what next happened was that Unconditional Unionists began to spy and report on their fellow Marylanders, some of whom were secessionists and others just people against whom some Unionist had a score to settle. Neighbors began having neighbors arrested. General Dix wrote to General McClellan on September 4:

> No secession flag has to the knowledge of the police been exhibited in Baltimore for many weeks, except a small paper flag displayed by a child from an upper window. It was immediately removed by them. They have been instructed to arrest any person who makes a public demonstration by word or deed in favor of the Confederate Government and I have

prohibited the exhibition in shop windows of rebel envelopes and music.

Indeed, these harsh actions were meant for everyone. Dix in the same report stated: "The old police when disbanded consisted of 416 persons. Twenty-seven are in our service. . . . There are some very mischievous, worthless fellows, but they are quiet. We only want a pretext for arresting them. They have up to this time been paid by the city." Finally he displayed his utter contempt for the mayor of Baltimore when he reported: "Yesterday I addressed a letter to the mayor ordering the payment to be discontinued. I think he will obey it. If he does not I shall arrest him and make a like order on the city comptroller who will obey."[34]

The effect of these orders on the secessionists of Maryland was devastating: their leading citizens arrested and elected officials ordered about; the federal military dismissing the power of the courts and establishing military law; homes and businesses arbitrarily searched and private property confiscated; their own police disbanded and citizens arrested for minor offenses. It was a bewildering set of circumstances. After the Confederate victory at First Manassas, a correspondent, William Wilkens Glenn, reported the following:

An advance of the Southern army was confidently expected. There was a strong revolutionary feeling throughout the State and hundreds of young men were ready to join Joe Johnson as soon as he appeared at the Annapolis Junction prior to an attack on Washington. . . . There was no attempt at individual organization or State Revolution, because that was thought inexpedient. A letter from Benjamin [Judah P. Benjamin, a member of the Confederate Cabinet] to Pratt [ex-Governor Pratt], advised him expressly not to make such an attempt then, for they [the Confederate Government] will be unable then to give the necessary assistance; but that all that was necessary for the present was to keep up a decided feeling in the State, so as to require the presence there of at least 20,000 Federal troops, which would thus be kept from Virginia.[35]

In these early weeks of the conflict, the war spirit ran high so this report could well be true. After all it was only July 1861. Later in the war, though, recruits were much harder to come by—for either side. But General Dix, commanding at Baltimore, requested reenforcements.

> The late reverse at Manassas has brought out manifestations of a most hostile and vindictive feeling in Annapolis, as well as Baltimore. Major-General Banks, on the evening of my arrival here, asked, at my suggestion, for four hundred cavalry. They would, for the special service required, be equal to a full regiment of infantry. I hope they may be furnished without delay. It is understood that a regiment of cavalry leaves New York tomorrow. Can I have a detachment of three or four companies from this regiment, with a field officer?[36]

Maryland was not quite subdued, and the federal military did not want to risk losing control, especially if the rumor of General Joseph P. Johnson's intended move toward Maryland proved true.

One final word is necessary on the Maryland legislature. It reconvened on July 30 in Frederick. By now, Baltimore, Annapolis, and most of the state were under some form of military control. Radcliffe concluded:

> Whatever hopes were entertained that Congress on assembling would secure a cessation of hostilities were shattered by the time the Maryland Legislature met on July 30, for the last of its memorable sessions. The energies of the United States Government were being exercised in the promotion of plans for the vigorous prosecution of the war. Baltimore had passed almost entirely under the management of the Federal authorities by the arrest of the police commissioners and Marshal Kane, and by the subsequent placing of the internal

government of the city under the actual control, or at least careful surveillance, of the officers of the United States troops stationed there. . . . The members of the Legislature on assembling . . . realized that any thought of opposition by them to the Federal administration was an idle one. . . . As it was, at the end of a week an adjournment took place. The spirit of hostility to the Federal administration was preserved in an intensified degree to the end.[37]

The General Assembly, in a final act of defiance, refused to fly the United States flag over its temporary statehouse in Frederick.

The administration since mid-April had been debating just what to do about that troublesome body. General Butler had been given orders to prevent any ordinance of secession from being passed and in September this order was still in effect. Maryland newspapers carried reports from towns all over the state of public meetings favoring secession. Lincoln's people, especially the military commanders and spies, read these with growing consternation. In addition, the administration received reports from its commanders in the field that secessionist military units were still drilling throughout Maryland. They also received secret reports regarding the leanings of members of the legislature. The Confederate victory at Manassas emboldened Maryland's secessionists, and with the legislature to meet on September 17, rumors circulated of a secret plan to pass an ordinance of secession in conjunction with a movement of the Confederate Army toward Maryland.

That was the final straw for the War Department. On September 11, Secretary Cameron issued the following order to General Banks, now commanding near Darnestown, a few miles from Frederick: "The passage of any act of secession by the

Legislature must be prevented. If necessary all or any part of the members must be arrested. Exercise your own judgment as to the time and manner, but do the work effectively."[38] A week before the legislature was scheduled to meet, orders went out to arrest members suspected of being secessionists. In league with the War Department were certain loyal Marylanders. William Seabrook, Frederick Schley, W. G. Snethen, S. W. Spencer, Jesse K. Hines, and George Vickers were among the most well-known. Lists of disloyal Marylanders were compiled, including a list of General Assembly members. Even eighteen months later, in the spring of 1863, when Confederate troops captured a Union messenger, among the papers seized were secret letters from Union men in Maryland to the War Department. One of the letters classified members of the legislature according to their political leanings. Members of the House of Delegates, had numbers from one to four next to their names, indicating the strength of their secessionist feelings, with four being the strongest. State senators were classified by letter: four S's meant the strongest secessionist and a U, of course, meant Unionist. The importance of these letters was that they documented for the War Department what it had been told by its spies.

General McClellan's official report to Secretary Seward on September 20, 1861, summarized the Maryland legislature. "The list I marked with you has been carefully revised and corrected by the Legislative journals, so that the propriety of the foregoing selection [arrests] is unquestionable. If the arrests are made the Senate will stand thus:

> Secessionists arrested, ... 11
> Secessionists absent from the State, . 1
> Secessionists at large, ... 3
> Union men at large, ... 6
> Doubtful men at large, ... 1
> Total 22

The House will stand thus:

Secessionists arrested, ... 40
Secessionists at large, ... 10
Union men at large, ... 15
Doubtful men at large, ... 8
Total . . . . 73[39]

McClellan's report and the secret letter did not match exactly. For instance, the secret letter listed twelve members of the House of Delegates as "Secessionists at large." But the point was unmistakably clear—the War Department's assessment of the Maryland legislature, based on the best intelligence of the day, was that the members were overwhelmingly secessionist. The federal command acted accordingly.

During this week, in addition to members of the legislature, federal authorities arrested Baltimore mayor George W. Brown and Henry May, congressman from the Fourth Legislative District. Those arrested were never formally charged or brought to trial. They were taken away to prisons in the North and held without bail or any form of due process under the law. Some of the state prisoners as they became known, generally those who were ill or otherwise nonthreatening, were released within a few days or weeks, but most were detained until November 1862, when they were released suddenly and without explanation.[40]

"The Maryland Arrests" had a deafening impact on Maryland secessionists, especially those who were less committed to the cause. W. G. Snethen, one of the War Department's spies in Baltimore, informed Secretary of State Seward on September 15:

I thank you in the name of every truly loyal man in Baltimore and in my own poor name too for your arrest of the traitors whom you have sent to Fortress Monroe. A good and a great work has been done. Rebellion has received a staggering blow. . . . The effect of these arrests must determine very rapidly the status of the floating population who are ever on the watch

> for the stronger side. I have already heard of cases in our favor.
> We are determined to prevent any rebel voting if he will not
> take the oath of allegiance. It is to be done by a system of
> challenging.[41]

With most of its members under arrest, the General Assembly
cancelled its scheduled meeting of September 17.

About the same time the Lincoln administration decided that
it had had enough with the Maryland legislature, it also decided
to clamp down on the pro-Southern press in Maryland. Several
Unconditional Unionists in Baltimore, emboldened by the presence of federal troops from whom they could seek protection,
increased their spying for the State Department. Their reports
constantly warned of the dangers of the pro-Southern press.
Allan Pinkerton, an agent of the State Department and later to
become the head of General McClellan's Secret Service, was sent
to Baltimore under an assumed name to assess the situation.

By early September plans were in place to control the Maryland press. These included arresting pro-Southern editors, refusing the use of the mails to distribute designated papers, and
finally orders to suspend permanently certain problem publications. In Baltimore, the government interfered with most of the
papers in one way or another. During the war no fewer than
nine Baltimore newspapers were suppressed, either temporarily
or permanently, and two of those were forced to stop publica-
tion because their editors had been incarcerated. Of the twelve
instances of such action by the government, eight were permanent closures and four were temporary suspensions for brief
periods. The suppressed Baltimore journals included the *South*,
the *Daily Exchange*, the *Maryland News Sheet*, the *Daily Republican*, the *Daily Gazette*, the *Evening Transcript*, the *Evening Bulletin*,
the *Evening Post* and the *Evening Loyalist*. Only the *American*, the
most loyal of all city papers, the *Clipper*, and the *Sun* were published
without interruption during the course of the conflict.[42]

For the most part, Maryland's pro-Southern newspapers kept up a continuous and persuasive attack on the administration and did not relent until forced to do so. Typical of their statements was this editorial from the *Daily Exchange* of April 15:

> We believe that right and justice are with our brethren of the South, and that the cause they represent and are defending is the cause of their domestic institutions, their chartered rights and their firesides. We look upon the Government which is assailing them as the representative, not of the Union, but of a malignant and sectional fanaticism, which takes the honored name of the Union in vain and has prostrated and is trampling on the Constitution. The war that Government has wantonly begun we regard as a wicked and desperate crusade, not only against the homes and rights of our Southern brethren, but against the fundamental American principle of self-government.[43]

Strong words indeed, and on the night of September 12, Francis Key Howard, editor of the *Daily Exchange,* was arrested, along with Thomas W. Hall, editor of the *South.* Howard was seized from his home in Baltimore and taken to Ft. McHenry where he joined his father—Charles Howard—in confinement. In a doubtless unintended coincidence, the younger Howard could gaze from his cell at the water beyond and reflect that his grandfather forty-seven years before to the day had been watching this fort when he became inspired to write "The Star Spangled Banner."[44]

In September 1861, Maryland ceased to be "the land of the free," but it was still "the home of the brave." As demonstrated by the courageous Howards, Marylanders refused to yield their freedoms and their Constitutional rights to the dictates of an overwhelming military force and as a result were carried off to prisons in the North. On September 14, William Wilkens Glenn

Maryland legislators Charles G. W. Macgill (left) and Henry M. Warfield (right) were arrested without charge in September 1861 and sent to federal prisons in the North. A highly respected physician from Western Maryland, Macgill joined the Army of Northern Virginia as a surgeon after his release in November 1862. (Courtesy Frederick D. Shroyer.)

recorded in his diary, "I was privately informed that I was to be arrested. I could easily have gotten away, but it was a point with me. . . . I determined to force the Government to have recourse to military power if they wished to muzzle free speech in Maryland. After dinner, McPhail came to the house with a small force and took me off."[45]

Editors and publishers across the state were put on notice: Comply with the administration's policies or face suspension or imprisonment or both. With these actions, the federal military established censorship over virtually every newspaper in the state. As the war progressed, military commanders were given increased authority to act on their own, and the press was subjected to harsher and more arbitrary actions than before.

Severn Teackle Wallis, prominent Balti-more lawyer and member of the General Assembly, was an ardent secessionist. Arrested in Baltimore in mid-September with the Maryland legislators, he was imprisoned at Fort McHenry and several Northern prisons. He autographed the signature card below while imprisoned at Fort Warren in June 1862. (Both courtesy Frederick D. Shroyer.)

☆

The final battle for the secession movement in Maryland was the gubernatorial election that fall. Historians have discussed and debated the election of November 6, 1861, at great length, and most have concluded that the federal government did play a deciding role in determining the outcome. Since April 15 the administration had shown through its actions, not words—military occupation of the state, suspension of the writ of habeas corpus, arbitrary arrests, disbanding the state legislature, suppression and censorship of the press—that it intended to secure Maryland to the Union by force. Faced with a scheduled election, it simply could not permit a party unfriendly to its cause to be freely elected in the state. To do so might undo all that it had thus far accomplished. As with the other great events of this period in Maryland, e.g. the riot in Baltimore on April 19, no attempt will be made in this work to cover each detail of the election, for that has been done quite adequately by several historians.[46]

By the fall of 1861, Maryland's political structure was in a veritable shambles, and every Marylander realized it. No one expected a normal election—and no one was disappointed on that count. First, the parties changed their names: the electorate was now faced with the Union Party, later in the war to become the party of the Unconditional Unionists, and a State Rights party, the former Democrats who would later become the Peace Party.

The Union Party nominated for governor Augustus W. Bradford, a relatively obscure politician and large slaveholder from Harford County. The State Rights or Peace Party, with many of their would-be leaders either out of the state or in jail, at first had trouble finding a candidate. Finally in October they nominated Benjamin C. Howard of Baltimore County. Howard, a

direct decendant of John Eager Howard of Revolutionary War
and Declaration of Independence fame, was widely known and
had instant appeal to a majority of Marylanders.

Governor Hicks and Lincoln's man, Bradford, suddenly fearing defeat in November, appealed to the administration in
Washington. Hicks requested assistance from Secretary Seward
and from the military commanders in Maryland, and help soon
arrived in the form of federal troops. These patrolled the polling
places to protect Union voters, assisted the election judges in
determining who was loyal enough to vote (a loyalty oath would
be required of certain voters), and even voted themselves when
needed. "Soldiers of the Maryland Federal Army in the field were
given voting privilege as well as Northern soldiers stationed in
Maryland on the pretence that they had been stationed in the
State sufficiently long to become citizens."[47]

The Lincoln administration had, by this time, made the decision
that a friendly party would be elected in Maryland and moved with
dispatch to see that it was done. Orders were issued to prevent any
disunionists in the state from interfering in the election and to
arrest any rebel returning to vote. The military authorities joined
forces with the Unionists. In Baltimore, General Dix remarked:
"We have shown that we can control Maryland by force. We now
wish to show that we can control it by the power of opinion."
Unfortunately, the power of opinion necessarily meant military
power. The Union Party would hardly be ousted from control so
long as federal troops were on hand to support it.[48]

Numerous accounts of voting irregularities marred the election. A correspondent of the *Maryland News Sheet* reported from
Annapolis that eight or nine thousand federal troops were
stationed in Anne Arundel County on election day, most of
them in Annapolis. There, nine enlisted seamen of the United
States Navy from the U.S.S. *Alleghany,* a receiving ship lying in
dock, came ashore to vote the Union ticket. Local electoral

judges challenged their votes on the grounds that they were nonresidents, but the protest was overruled. According to the correspondent, those nine sailors spelled defeat for the State Rights senatorial candidate of Anne Arundel, who lost the election by six votes, and the State Rights candidate for the House of Delegates who lost by four.[49]

Voting in the 1860s, before the Australian ballot, was a highly pubic affair. No booths or curtains shielded the voter, who simply walked into a room, picked up a ballot, marked it, and dropped it in a box or handed it to an election judge. In some cases there was no secrecy at all, for the ballots were striped or otherwise clearly marked in such a way so that the election judge knew how the man had voted. Thus, election judges could tell immediately who was winning a given election.

The results of this one were so unusual as to be unbelievable. Bradford won with 57,502 votes to Howard's 26,070, and remember that only a few weeks before November 6 both Hicks and Bradford were concerned they would lose. Unionists captured control of the House of Delegates, sixty-eight to six. In pro-Confederate Southern Maryland the *St. Mary's Beacon,* dripping sarcasm, commented: "Mr. Bradford, the war candidate, has been elected—we think they call it—by thirty or three hundred thousand majority, we have forgotten which."[50]

A digression is warranted here to compare the results of the November 1860 election (the last free election in the state) with the outcome a year later. In November 1860 the results were as follows:

Lincoln	2,294
Douglas	5,966
Breckinridge	42,482
Bell	41,760

Breckinridge represented the most pronounced stance for the South and it was possible, but hardly plausible, that any number of his ardent supporters, 42,482 strong, would now go over and vote for the Lincoln-backed candidate, Augustus Bradford. The Bell vote, 41,760, was the moderate or conservative Southern vote and included many, if not most, of the slaveholders. How many of this group now voted for the Lincoln-backed candidate is open to question, but the number was probably not large. If from the presidential election of 1860, we add all of the vote for Lincoln (2,294), all of the vote for Douglas (5,966), 10 percent of the vote for Breckinridge (4,248), and 50 percent of the vote for Bell (20,880), the total is only 33,388 potential votes for Bradford. One can play with the numbers in various ways but it seems clear that Bradford could not have garnered 57,502 legitimate votes. The numbers suggest that this election was rigged.

But what about the views of Maryland historians? Four are presented in an attempt to establish some kind of consensus. Charles B. Clark thought that the manner of Bradford's victory was the least satisfactory feature of his entire career, public or private. J. Thomas Scharf was more critical:

Soldiers were stationed at the polls in nearly all the polling places throughout the State. Many hundreds of citizens were arrested in the various counties and in the City of Baltimore, without the slightest pretext, and evidently for the mere purpose of deterring their neighbors and political friends from attempting to exercise their rights. . . . The election was a shameless mockery, and its results were but the work of fraud and violence. The 'Union' candidate for governor was declared elected, he having received in the City of Baltimore 17,922 votes, while the democratic candidate was said to have polled but 3,347 votes. In the State the entire 'Union' ticket was elected by a majority of 31,438 votes. Small as the vote was, it is a notorious fact that an immense number of illegal votes were everywhere cast for the Administration candidates. Massachusetts soldiers were known to have boasted in Boston that they voted on that day in Baltimore, as often as they pleased . . . and a governor, and a large portion of the Legislature and the judiciary of the State, went into office with the knowledge that they owed their elevation to power to those who controlled the military powers then within our borders.[51]

Radcliffe, who had personally interviewed many of the actual participants in the election concluded that the Lincoln administration had "put forward great efforts to secure an endorsement at the polls; and indeed the election was held directly under the supervision of the United States Government." General Dix in Baltimore had instructed election judges "to satisfy themselves as to the qualifications of the voters," to closely question voters about their residence and citizenship in order to "detect traitors and without any violation of the constitution or laws of Maryland . . . prevent the pollution of the ballot boxes by their votes." This discouraged not only the strong pro-Confederate vote, but the "many others who had never allied themselves with this cause, but who, as a result of the general feverishness of the times and the personal animosities thereby engendered" might have come to the polls but did not. Taking into account the large number of Maryland citizens who had crossed the Potomac to wear Confederate gray, Radcliffe concluded that "the election of November 6, 1861, cannot be regarded as even an approximately accurate expression of public sentiment in Maryland."[52]

And finally, Harold W. Manakee noted that to ensure a large majority for the Union Party, three Maryland infantry regiments were given furloughs to return home and vote. Polling places displayed proclamations by military commanders requesting "all persons to report to the police anyone trying to vote who had engaged in hostile acts against the United States, or who had helped those in arms against the government." Armed troops patrolled the polls, and watched non-Maryland soldiers cast their votes in Annapolis and Baltimore. "The election set the pattern for all others during the war." Protesting that the Constitution gave states the right to manage elections, the Peace Party protested loudly but to no avail. Military officials ignored the protests, the Union Party won a sweeping victory, and Augustus W. Bradford, a strong supporter of the federal government, became governor.[53]

Completely consistent with its policy toward the state since April 15, the Lincoln administration did what it had to do in the election to keep Maryland securely tied to the Union. "Maryland had been compelled to cooperate with the United States Government by force of arms. Whatever may have been the inclination of the majority of the people in the state, certainly nearly all the officials, Hicks being the most conspicuous exception, had been avowedly out of sympathy with Lincoln's course."[54]

In the last few months of his term, Governor Hicks had turned completely on his former associates. On September 20 he wrote General Banks, "We have some of the product of your order here in the persons of some eight or ten members of the State Legislature, soon, I learn, to depart for healthy quarters. We see the good fruit already produced by the arrests. We can no longer mince matters with these desperate people. I concur in all you have done."[55] And on November 12, regarding the potential early release of the Maryland state prisoners, he wrote Seward:

I beg that you be particular . . . to release Teackle Wallis, T. Parkin Scott, H. M. Warfield, &c., will be to give us as much trouble here as would the liberation of Mayor Brown, George P. Kane, the police commissioners of Baltimore, and other like spirits to them. We are going right in Maryland and I beg that nothing be done to prevent what I have long desired and labored for, viz, the identification of Maryland with the Government proper.[56]

Thus, he urged that Mayor Brown and Marshal Kane, two men

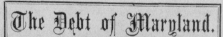

Remember,—men of Maryland,
    You have a debt to pay,
A debt which years of patience
    Will never wear away :
Which must be paid, at last,—although
    Our dearest blood it cost—
A debt which *shall* be paid unto
    The very uttermost.

We owe for confidence betrayed,
    By those we trusted best ;
The sword we gave them, to defend,
    They turned against our breast !
For spies that noted down our words,
    The while they shared our bread,
For *hounds* that even dared disturb,
    The quiet of the dead !

We owe for all the love they lied,
    The wolfish hate they showed,
For all these glittering bayonets
    That meet us on the road ;
For black suspicion, deadlier far
    Than flash of Northern swords,
For treason threatened at our hearths,
    And poison at our boards.

For many a deed of darkness done
    Beneath their " Stripes and Stars,"
For women outraged in their homes,
    And fired on in the cars ;
For those black tiers of cannon trained,
    To bear on Baltimore—
We owe for friends in prison kept,
    And DAVIS in his gore !

Wrongs such as these,—aye,—more than these,
    Make up our fearful debt,
And many a gallant heart has sworn,
    It shall be settled yet !
Each moment near and nearer brings
    That solemn reckoning day :
And when it comes—*as come it must*
    Remember—and repay !

BALTIMORE, *October*, 16, 1861.   H.

Poems and songs expressed Maryland's Confederate sentiment and supported the cause. "The Debt of Maryland" is noteworthy because it was published on October 16, 1861—long after federal troops had occupied the state and outlawed such expressions of disloyalty. (Courtesy, Frederick D. Shroyer.)

who probably saved his life in those dark days of April, be kept in prison, even after the state was firmly under control of the federal military. It was little wonder that so many Marylanders of the day despised their governor.

So ended the secession movement in Maryland. From April to September 1861 the Maryland legislature was composed of men who leaned strongly toward the South and who desired secession. But following the arrest of its pro-Southern members in September and their replacement in November with men loyal to the Union, the legislature adhered to a policy of supporting the Union and passed stringent measures to curtail the liberties of its citizens. "The people of Maryland, however, were not fully subservient to the Federal government. . . . Only by constant watchfulness and the actual presence of Federal military power was Maryland saved for the Union and kept in step with its major purposes until the end of the conflict."[57]

The power of the federal armies forced Maryland to stay in the Union.

6

The Military Issue:
More Than Just Numbers

'Twas in the dying of the day,
The darkness grew so still;
The drowsy pipe of evening birds
Was hushed upon the hill;
Athwart the shadows of the vale
Slumbered the men of might,
And one lone sentry paced his rounds,
To watch the camp that night.

James Ryder Randall

Over the years, those who have discussed and written about Maryland and the question of secession often have cited the numbers of Marylanders who fought for the North as a litmus test of Maryland's loyalty to the Union. We have fairly accurate data on the Union side, as contained in the *Official Records*, and we can make a reasonable estimate of the number who served in the Confederate forces. These figures show that about twice as many Marylanders fought for the North as for the South. It is certainly legitimate to ask, then, whether this was some indication of the true feeling of the state relative to the sentiment for or against secession. Of course, there is no way to prove categorically that there was a linkage at all. But it is important to examine this issue because the argument is so often used. In most cases, arguments over the numbers of Maryland volunteers fall prey to an apples-to-oranges comparison; that is, they compare Marylanders with Marylanders-plus-others and volunteers with volunteers-plus-others. This chapter attempts to establish a basis for an apples-to-apples comparison between Marylanders who volunteered for either the North or the South and then make the comparison based on this rationale.

First, we must establish the basis for discussion. In the election of 1860 Maryland closely identified herself with the South. That election, unlike those that had closely preceded it and those that came after the federal occupation, was relatively free—from election day rowdyism, from federal military intervention, and from federal officials attempting to manipulate election results. The election of 1860 therefore offers a window through which one can obtain as nearly as possible an untainted view of the true feelings of Marylanders. Chapter 5 demonstrated how the influence of the federal government could skew election results, as in the case of the gubernatorial election of 1861, in which the results are simply not believable. Likewise, in discussing Marylanders who joined the armies, we must restrict our examination to the year 1861 so that we can get the most unbiased or uncluttered view of the numbers of men who took up arms for one side or the other out of conviction. Eighteen sixty-one was the year of the enthusiastic volunteer. "The war was greeted in its first few weeks almost as a festival. Everybody seemed relieved. People went out and celebrated, both in the North and in the South. There were parades, bands playing, flags flying; people seemed almost happy. Large numbers of troops were enlisted; as a matter of fact, again in both North and South, more men offered themselves than could be handled."[1]

After 1861 it is impossible to determine who actually volunteered. In 1862 the Confederacy, and in 1863 the Union, had resorted to conscription. States and counties also offered bounties to men who enlisted, and those with means paid others to enlist in their stead. To best determine Maryland's stance in the conflict, it is absolutely essential to count only those who joined up because they believed in a cause and voluntarily offered their services. Also, we must define *Marylander* and deal with the issue of new residents of the state. This is the only way to get a reasonable comparison.

An accurate number of Marylanders who volunteered for the North—as opposed to the number who enlisted for bounties or through conscription—is extremely hard to obtain. Even during the first months of the war, when patriotic fervor and enthusiasm were very high, the number of Marylanders who really volunteered to serve in the Union army is questionable. No doubt reflecting Marylanders' unwillingness to raise a hand against the South, the state was "particularly lax and deficient" in filling her early quotas. Lincoln's April 15 call for troops established a quota for Maryland of 3,123, but the state recruited not a single soldier. Lincoln issued a second call on May 3 for 500,000 men for three years, and Maryland ultimately raised 9,355 men of the 15,578 requested as her quota. In Baltimore especially there was great resistance to joining up. The *Baltimore Daily Exchange*, whose sympathies lay decidedly with the South, described Northern recruiting as an "up-hill business," and claimed "every deception was practised to induce the citizenry to enlist," which in turn led roughly one-half of the enlistees to desert.[2] In contrast to the overwhelming response to Lincoln's call for troops from the Northern states, this reaction offers a sense of how Marylanders felt. Only one group established itself as enthusiastic Northern volunteers—the newly immigrated Germans of Baltimore were the most avid Unionists, especially the various Turner societies (liberal German political organizations). "Most of the Turners, who had formed the bulk of Baltimore's insignificant Republican element before the war, immediately joined the Union army."[3]

However, by 1862 the picture of volunteering was anything but muddy. Various forms of enrollment were instituted to meet federally imposed quotas. Federal troops went from house to house searching for recruits. Undesirables were rounded up and enlisted. Enrollment stations began to pay sizeable bounties to entice men to sign up. A draft was instituted, and citizens were permitted to pay substitutes to take their place if drafted. Finally, beginning in May 1863 blacks, both free and slave, were recruited with a promise of good pay or freedom at war's end.

As early as December 1861, the War Department complained about the quality of the recruits. "The large number of enlisted men discharged on 'certificates of disability' has attracted the notice of the General-in-Chief. . . . Evidence is abundant, as attested by the records of the Adjutant-General's Office, that many men have been enlisted who were 'unfit for service' prior to or at date of enlistment."[4] General Orders No. 104 unsuccessfully attempted to halt the practice of enlisting undesirables or those unfit for service by requiring recruiting officers to forfeit from their own pockets any expenses incurred by the army whenever unfit men were mustered in.

> Several of the early volunteer units were equally menacing to the public welfare. Composed of the state's most undesirable element, the members of these organizations were united in quest of excitement and plunder rather than fulfilling a patriotic duty. Two companies of volunteers, styling themselves the Governor's Guard, took up residence at the Zion Church of Baltimore. This group conducted itself in such a disorderly manner that its arms were seized, and the volunteers were placed under the custody of the corporate authorities.[5]

In August 1861, Congress passed a law authorizing a bounty of up to $100 to be paid to each able-bodied recruit. The law was later rescinded, but by 1864 bounties from $250 to $500 were commonplace.[6] That was a considerable sum in 1860. Three hundred dollars was a very fair year's income for an unskilled laborer. "Even a skilled mechanic would not make twice that much money in a year, and in the ordinary course of things, never actually saw as much as $300 in cash."[7] Large numbers of poor or destitute individuals volunteered in order to collect sizeable amounts of cash, and bounties remained indispensable to enticing recruits throughout the war. One enterprising young recruiting official from Baltimore City opened an office in Cumberland and offered volunteers the new Baltimore City bounty of $142 in addition to Alleghany County's bounty of $100, which gave them the "princely total" of $242.[8] Occasionally officials overreached in their efforts to secure recruits. By the fall of 1861 volunteers were induced with promises of a monetary reward at the end of their service. The funds were not there, but officials hoped their promises would force the state or federal government to appropriate them.[9]

Next came the draft. On July 17, 1862, Congress enacted the Militia Law, which gave president the authority to call state militias into federal service for nine months and defined the militia as every able-bodied man between eighteen and forty-five. On the heels of a call for 300,000 men in July, the government called for an additional draft of 300,000 nine-month men. So unpopular did in prove in some parts of the country that federal troops eventually had to go house-to-house collecting men who had been selected but failed to report. The threat of a draft did not surprise Marylanders—it had been discussed for months—and the War Department tipped its hand by authorizing the arrests of persons suspected of discouraging enlistments evading military service. Despite this safeguard, in Maryland "an alarming exodus of citizens began. From Baltimore alone, it was reported that in a week about 1,000 persons left in route to Canada and other British possessions. . . . Hundreds of young men were preparing to cross the Potomac to join the Confederate Army, and secessionists openly declared that they would die by their firesides rather than fight the South."[10]

Another complex issue relative to the draft was that the federal government permitted a citizen to pay someone else to take his place in the event his name was drawn in the draft. When Maryland did not meet her quotas for the July and August calls, the long-expected draft took place throughout the state on October 15, 1862. "Those drawn were notified to present themselves at the place of rendezvous within five days. . . . Substitutes were accepted in place of those unwilling to serve in person; and a lively business was done in that traffic, prices ranging from $300 to $700. Many of these substitutes, escaping from the camp of instruction, sold their services several times over."[11] All over the nation paid volunteers and bounty men began to appear. The term bounty jumper was applied to the man who sold his services over and over. A great many substitutes also went to war. "At least 75,000 men were hired by drafted civilians. In addition, about 42,000 men were paid to go into the army as substitutes."[12] An interesting picture of the Union Volunteer emerged by 1862.

The recruitment of black soldiers is excluded from this analysis because, except for those who served in the navy, they were not recruited until 1863. However, it is noteworthy that almost 19 percent of Maryland's Union volunteers were black, and that they supplied six regiments of U.S. Colored Troops. Free blacks were promised good wages and the means to support themselves, and slaves were promised freedom upon enlistment. Some over-zealous federal officers confiscated slaves despite vigorous protests by their owners, and by late 1864 a board or commission was established to award compensation to loyal slaveowners for slaves so enlisted. The War Department reported that over 2,000 claims had been received by October 1864.[13]

Finally, there is the question of how many Marylanders actually served in the federal army. Throughout the war, War Department requests for additional troops poured into Maryland, but state and federal officials never seemed able to agree on the number of Maryland troops in Union blue. "The existence of both state-inspired and federal-directed recruitment caused constant confusion and uncertainty."[14]

However, there was one certainty regarding Maryland's Union volunteers: by the summer of 1862 there were very few men coming forward of their own free will to enlist in the Union army. Governor Bradford and his staff were alarmed at the prospect of not being able to meet the state's quotas, and the General Assembly appropriated money for bounties. Essentially, by the closing months of 1861 the number of volunteers was down to a trickle. Again, the reason we must deal solely with the year 1861 for our comparison is this: if we are to compare a volunteer for the North with a volunteer for the South, the term *volunteer* must be precise—a true, un-coerced, coming-forward-on-one's-own-free-will enlistee. Conscripts, substitutes, and bounty men have no bearing on this discussion.

The other issue concerning this comparison is the matter of just how many Union volunteers were in fact Marylanders. We will define "Marylander" as someone who was born (and thus likely raised) in the state. Bradley T. Johnson wrote of Maryland Union volunteers: "These first forces raised for the Union in Maryland were, with the exception of the First regiment, mainly composed of foreigners, aliens by birth and aliens to the institutions, ideals and motives that for nine generations had formed the character of Marylanders. . . . The First Maryland under Kenly was the only Maryland regiment on the Union side."[15] Johnson was a Confederate officer and his view, expressed after the war, needs at least some substantiation or some corroboration by other historians.

First, a review of the numbers from the census of 1860 as reported in chapter 1. Maryland did have a large number of foreign immigrants. The census reported nearly 78,000 foreign-born out of a total white population of 600,000, or 13 percent. Another 41,000 Marylanders had been born out of the state. In 1860 then, nearly one out of five people living in Maryland had not been born there. Most had settled in Baltimore or Western Maryland. Many of these non-Maryland born were truly different—they dressed differently, spoke differently, and indeed acted differently. Immigrants particularly were not well liked.

> The Irish, even more than the Germans, called unfavorable attention to themselves by their fighting, rioting, drunkenness, and squalor. Holidays and Sundays were favorite occasions for brawling. Toughs and rowdies did not confine the use of clubs, stones, dirks, pistols, and guns to each other, but turned them against innocent and peaceable citizens for reasons of sport, spite, and robbery.[16]

About two-thirds of the foreign- and out-of-state-born residents of Maryland in 1860 were Germans. There were two distinct groups: the Germans of Western Maryland, who had immigrated to the state largely from Pennsylvania (some had been in Maryland for decades by 1860); and the Germans of Baltimore, most of whom had recently immigrated to Maryland from Europe. Both groups were decidedly pro-Union. The primary difference between them was that most of the Western Maryland Germans had been born in America and the Germans of Baltimore were newly arrived people who had been born in Germany. Called "Forty-Eighters" because they had fled Europe during the German Revolution of 1848, they at first considered their stay in America as a temporary arrangement. They adapted slowly, learned English reluctantly, and "did little or nothing to acquaint themselves with American conditions." They cared little about the constitutional aspects of the war. "Older Americans were influenced—frequently in favor of the South—by the fact that the conflict hinged, among other things, also on the question as to whether the individual state could act as it pleased or whether it had to surrender important rights to the federal government." But the German immigrants cared little about states rights. "It made no difference to them whether they lived in Pennsylvania, Wisconsin, or Texas."[17]

These Germans formed a large part of Maryland's Unionists. During the secession crisis, Germans in Frederick County held large Union meetings, and the "Brengle Home Guard" had organized there even before the legislature retreated to Frederick from Annapolis. Captain B. H. Schley organized Frederick County's first Union regiment. The only Republican newspaper in Maryland to advocate and energetically support Lincoln's election was Baltimore's German daily, *Der Wecker*. Leopold Blumenburg of Baltimore raised the 5th Maryland Regiment and thereby earned the lasting emnity of secessionists in the city, who openly threatened his life. After an unsuccessful attack on his house, it had to be guarded by police. "If on the other hand one examines the troop lists of the Maryland regiments who fought on the side of the South, the absence of German names is most striking."[18]

The foreign-born and out-of-state born residents were citizens of Maryland under the law, but they were different people—different in their ways, different in their outlook and expectations, and certainly out of step, politically, with other Marylanders of the day. Perhaps Bradley Johnson was right when he exclaimed, "They were good men, but they were not Marylanders."[19]

Again, to make an apples-to-apples comparison we need to

define the apple carefully. The argument can certainly be made that those born and raised in a given locale are more apt to know the customs, interests, and politics of the region and thereby represent the true feelings of a given area. This is pertinent to our discussion. It should be noted, however, that most of the Northern states had large foreign-born populations, as did some Southern states, for example Louisiana and Texas. Furthermore, westward migration in the antebellum years meant that many residents of newer states in the Midwest and South had been born elsewhere.

The mountain people of Alleghany County (which in 1860 comprised what is now Alleghany and Garrett Counties) were basically of German stock (there was also a sizeable immigrant population from Great Britain among the coal miners) but they were a bit different from the Germans of Frederick and Washington Counties. The Alleghany Countians were coal miners who had come from Pennsylvania and other Northern states. They were aligned politically with other mountaineers— whether they resided in Maryland, Virginia, Tennessee, or Alabama. They too, were strongly pro-Union and, in fact, supplied Lincoln with many of his votes in 1860. They responded to Lincoln's call for troops enthusiastically and for the duration of the war furnished more than their share of the troop quotas for Maryland. "They were all stalwart Republicans, when it took nerve to be a Republican in a slave state." In 1862 Alleghany County's quota was 872 men; 1,463 volunteered for duty, many from the mining area.[20] Western Maryland was, indeed, the Union stronghold in the state.

In contrast, let us now look at the Marylanders who volunteered for the South.[21] Our discussion will focus on the difficulty faced by Marylanders who wished to enlist in the Confederate army, the timing of the majority of those enlistments, and a review of the backgrounds of Marylanders who chose to wear gray.

In the early days of 1861, before the war actually began, the Confederate government set up a recruiting office in Baltimore. When war commenced they actively encouraged enlistments throughout the state. Their efforts met with considerable success but were short-lived—Northern troops rapidly occupying the state shut down this activity as quickly as they could. Most of the Maryland Guard units were pro-Southern, and several of those units went south early on, almost en masse. Many of their captains soon became officers in the Confederate army—Steuart, Tilghman, Trimble, and Johnson to name a few. But after the first few weeks of the war, it was impossible for Marylanders to enlist easily in the Confederate army. There simply were no mechanisms in place for them to use. Marylanders had to find their way to Harper's Ferry or Richmond on their own and at their own expense. They went singly or in small bands, often joining the first unit they encountered. Sometimes they enlisted with a friend's or a relative's unit, and some even enlisted as Virginians. Although Marylanders managed to form a small "Maryland Line" of infantry, cavalry, and artillery in the Confederate army, most fought with units from other states and left no record.[22]

It is impossible to know the exact number of Marylanders who served the South, but one thing is absolutely clear—they were true volunteers. In 1861, there were no inducements, no forms of coercion, no bounties, no promises of one kind or another. "They crossed the Potomac simply as patriotic volunteers, desiring to serve a cause in which they deeply believed and for which they were willing to endure hardship and sacrifice their lives."[23] In fact, as the summer and fall of 1861 unfolded, the Maryland Confederate volunteer had more and more difficulty and some real danger just getting out of the state.

Isaac Ridgway Trimble took command of the largely pro-Southern Maryland volunteers after the April 19 riots in Baltimore and disbanded the militiamen shortly before General Butler marched federal troops into the city. Trimble later became a brigadier general in the Army of Northern Virginia and served with distinction under the legendary Stonewall Jackson. (Courtesy Daniel D. Hartzler.)

This leads to the second issue which is important to our discussion of Maryland Confederates—the matter of timing. In the early weeks of the war, it was relatively easy for the Marylander to make his way south, either with a unit or as an individual. But as the year went on, federal troops cut off many, if not most, of the routes to the South. By the fall of 1861, there were tens of thousands of federal troops in Maryland, and they controlled virtually all major roads, bridges and railroads. They patrolled the Maryland side of the Potomac, and federal gunboats became more numerous and more aggressive in patrolling the Chesapeake Bay as well as the Potomac River.[24]

Within a few months orders were issued to the federal commanders in Maryland to arrest men attempting to leave the state. By the end of 1861, the federal government had complete control of the state, from its political apparatus to its roads, railroads, rivers, and bays. The large majority of Marylanders who joined the Confederate army did so in 1861.

Finally, a comment on the backgrounds of Maryland Confederates. Daniel Hartzler pointed out that the majority of Maryland's political, military, and educational leaders were pro-Southern. He also demonstrated that virtually every old-line Maryland family was represented in the Confederate army. To be sure, the sons of the large slaveholders went south in overwhelming numbers. Even the Unionist war governor, Augustus Bradford, a very wealthy large slaveholder, had a son who was an officer in the Confederate army. But as noted in chapter 2, there were only 2,580 large slave-holders in the state. Thus, it was the sons of the old-line Maryland families, many of whom owned no slaves, who filled the ranks in the Confederate army. "As the roll of those who saw service under the Stars and Bars is read, it is astonishing to note an almost complete roster of the names of the men who gave luster to and fought beneath the folds of the Star-Spangled Banner during the Revolution and in the War of 1812."[25] These names represented the great middle-class of the state in 1861, just as they did in 1776 and 1812. It was the old-line families of the state, slaveholding and non-slaveholding alike, that lined up in support of the South.

At the beginning of the conflict, both sides thought it would be a short war—perhaps a battle or two—before the country would find a means to effect reunion, or independence. Enthusiasm was high. The youthful war spirits soared. "When the young recruits on both sides first got to camp, they were all in a great hurry to get to the front. A lot of them were scared the war was going to end before they got into action."[26] But by 1862, after the first few battles—and the first large batches of casualties—a more somber mood engulfed both North and South. This had a dramatic impact on volunteering, and both sides instituted drafts and other forms of enlistment. The volunteers of 1861, both North and South, were closest to the real thing.

In summary, 1861 is crucial to this analysis for two reasons. First, in regard to Maryland's Union volunteers, from 1862 until the end of the war Union forces drafted, conscripted, bought, and cajoled so many Marylanders to meet the state's quotas that it is simply impossible to determine how many had lived in the state for any length of time and how many of those volunteered without inducement for purely patriotic reasons. Some, including Bradley Johnson, have argued that they were very, very few in number. The *Official Records* support this view by documenting the extreme difficulty Maryland had in meeting its quotas.

Second, with regard to the Confederate volunteers, after 1861 Maryland was so closely controlled by federal forces that it was extremely difficult and downright dangerous to attempt to go south. Thus the number of enlistees who enrolled after that year was very small. It is also worth repeating in regard to both North and South, that after 1861 early excitement and optimism had turned to dismay and indeed horror as the casualty lists mounted. By mid-1862 fewer men wanted to go to war, as the draft riots which soon engulfed many Northern cities so clearly proved.

A comparison of volunteers provides the following conclusion: In 1861, the only year that patriotic volunteerism can be measured reasonably for either side, approximately 9,000 Marylanders volunteered to fight for the Union. That number is dwarfed by the waves of Marylanders who, taking a dangerous course, traveled south to enlist in Confederate forces. Most scholars agree that between 15,000 and 25,000 Marylanders served in gray. If one takes the mid-point of 20,000 and discounts it by 10 percent to represent the few who were able to reach Southern lines after 1861, the approximate figure of Maryland Confederate volunteers in the first critical months of the war is 18,000, or *twice* the number of Union volunteers. Again, it is worth remembering that the Union volunteer merely had to walk down the street to the nearest recruiting station to enlist, while the Confederate volunteer had to travel many miles at his own expense and at some real personal risk to enlist with Southern forces.

Marylanders never, during the entire course of the war, responded with anything like enthusiasm to Union calls for volunteers. Maryland's record was the worst of any state—of the 70,965 troops requested by the War Department, only 46,638 were furnished. More than 8,700 were slaves and free blacks recruited into the United States Colored Troops.[27] When the Army of Northern Virginia entered the state in June 1863, Governor Bradford declared an emergency and urgently appealed to Marylanders to come to the defense of their state. He called for 10,000 volunteers in this moment of crisis. "Fortunately Lee's armies did not molest the state at large as they passed through en route to the decisive conflict at Gettysburg. Only 1,615 men answered the call for 10,000 in Maryland."[28]

From the first, the eagerness with which pro-Southern Marylanders voted with their feet and crossed over to Confederate service contrasted sharply with pro-Union support that seemed almost ambivalent. In 1861 Maryland was called upon to furnish more than 18,000 volunteers of which only about half were forthcoming. Prior to the August 4, 1862 call, Maryland's quotas exceeded 27,000, but less than half that number were recruited. Of those 13,343 volunteers 76 percent hailed from Alleghany, Frederick, Washington and Cecil Counties and Baltimore City. Five of Maryland's twenty-two counties, including Baltimore City, furnished more than three-fourths of its Union volunteers. Of the more than 4,000 men reported to have been drafted as of January 1, 1863, almost 3,000 had failed to appear. "Of the draftees who did come forth, about 1,000 offered substitutes, and only approximately 200 Marylanders submitted to personal service." Maryland's Union recruiting officers found it necessary to recruit in Washington and in some Northern states, especially Pennsylvania. In all, Maryland furnished 42,713 men to the

Pennsylvania. In all, Maryland furnished 42,713 men to the Union army. "It is necessary, however, to use the general term 'men' rather than 'Marylanders' when speaking of that State's volunteers. Rebels, aliens, and out-of-State substitutes were all enlisted by Maryland, and their number was legion."[29]

The precise numbers of Marylanders who patriotically volunteered for the Union and Confederate armies will never be known. But what seems clear is that a sizeable portion, if not a majority, of the men who were counted as Maryland volunteers in the Union army were, in fact, not volunteers at all, and many were not Marylanders. On the other hand, the sons of Maryland who went South were both—they represented the non-slaveholding, old-line families of the state as well as the wealthy, slaveholding oligarchy. And without question, they were truly volunteers.

Silver cross worn by Maryland volunteers in Confederate service.
(Courtesy, Daniel D. Hartzler.)

7

A Matter of Economics

By blue Patapsco's billowy dash
The tyrant's war-shout comes,
Along with the cymbal's fitful clash
And the growl of his sullen drums;
We hear it, we heed it, with vengeful thrills,
And we shall not forgive or forget—
There's faith in the streams, there's hope in the hills,
"There's life in the Old Land yet!"

James Ryder Randall

Many students of the war have debated the issue of whether Maryland, or for that matter any Southern state, would have been better off, economically speaking, seceding from the North. Would Maryland's trade and commerce have expanded or suffered if she cast her fate with the Southern Confederacy? By 1860 the economic statistics were overwhelmingly in favor of the North. Most of the trade and commerce was there, most of the manufacturing and capital necessary to expand trade and commerce. Indeed, most of the federal government's disbursements for internal improvements—roads, canals, and railroads needed for expansion of trade and commerce—were directed at and spent in the North. Thirty years after the war, Edward Ingle wrote that many of the economic disadvantages under which the South labored were traceable to "the compromises of the Constitution." They permitted the North to enjoy "a steady increase in power of population and ready capital, notwithstanding its natural impediments." A growing population led to greater representation in Congress, which "made it more and more impossible for the South to interrupt its plans for expansion involving the direct aid of the general government." The North was thus able to "monopolize native commerce, and to lead trade through its own gates."[1] Congress, under the firm control of Northern states by 1860, stacked laws and regulations in favor of their section. Protective tariffs and the Bank of the United States also fostered Northern manufactures. "With these two discriminating institutions commerce soon became concentrated in Northern cities. Benefited by the high duties, aided by the United States Bank and by long credit, Northern merchants were able to outstrip Southern importers and at the expense of the latter. Commerce thus being centered in Northern cities, nearly all revenues collected were retained in those places."[2]

Southern businessmen were aware of what was going on, and some twenty-odd years before the war they began holding commercial conventions in an attempt to address some of the issues affecting the lack of trade and commerce in the South. Leading men of the era—Thomas P. Kettell and J. D. B. DeBow were two of the notables—wrote extensively on the subject, pointing out that the South had to develop more of its own trade and commerce and not rely so heavily on the North. According to Kettell, this sectional movement alarmed many in the North, for it portended a possible loss of business.

The movement for Southern economic independence that got under way in the 1830s filled the merchants of New York with fear, not because they were worried by the Southern

Commercial Conventions but because of the influence of the abolition movement. The merchants feared that, because of the sectional controversy over slavery, New York printed on a box of merchandize would symbolize to the Southerners hostility to slavery and Southern Rights.[3]

After the war, historians examined the statistics and analyzed the North's economic advantage over the South in great detail. The works of Herbert Wender and Edward Ingle are of particular interest relative to this topic.[4] The data seemed clearly in favor of the North, and it must have been difficult to argue the economic advantage for a border state like Maryland to leave its favorable Northern commercial relations to join less secure Southern ones, that is, if one merely looked at past statistics and attempted to infer future benefit or lack thereof from past methods of conducting business. In 1930, Wender concluded:

> Concentration of capital, the national bank, protection to industry, the spread of free labor and centralization of government were the forces aligned against decentralization, free trade, and slavery. The Northern States were rapidly gaining wealth, power and national control, while the Southern States were at a relative standstill and forced to compromise.[5]

Some put forward the argument that under a Southern Confederacy new methods of conducting business would have evolved and accrued future benefit to a given region, state, or city. W. Jefferson Buchanan, a former Maryland governor, published widely on this subject during the early months of the war, arguing that Baltimore could become the leading port of the South if Maryland joined the Confederacy. Others argued that the expanding railroad system was drawing Maryland to the West, which was largely pro-North. But Edward C. Smith in 1927 countered by arguing that Maryland had not been particularly fortunate in its commercial relations with the West because of the barrier formed by the Alleghanies. But when the Baltimore and Ohio Railroad reached a terminus on the Ohio River in 1858, a few years before the war, "a much greater area was made tributary to the commercial centers of Maryland." Change was forthcoming, but by 1861 it was too soon to be readily apparent.[6]

Nevertheless, any thoughts of how Maryland's economy would have fared had the state joined the Confederacy are speculative at best. Rather, this chapter will deal with the more relevant issue of whether Maryland businessmen were pro-South or pro-North and what impact their support had on the secession movement. It is important to look at this group. Not only were they influential, but these were the men who controlled trade, commerce, and manufacturing and, thereby, much of the economic life of the state. They thrived in times of political stability and had the most to lose when that stability collapsed. Thus, the support of the mercantile class was key to Maryland's stance for or against secession.[7]

This placing of one's convictions on the line, of risking all for the belief in principle, is a sentiment worth examining. In no other state of the South was this issue of risk so immediate. The federal capital was located on its border. Maryland had a long and exposed border with the North, and was thus a potential battleground. Ingle, using Virginia as his example, wrote:

> The slaveholding States that were slow to join the Confederacy, or that failed to do so, cannot be accused of a deficiency of courage or of conviction. The best of them all, probably, Virginia, must have known that it had less to gain and more to lose materially by entering the Confederacy than any other State in the South. But such a consideration had little weight at the secret meeting of the convention of April, 1861. The call for troops to be employed against the farther South left Virginia the choice of joining in the coercive measures of the

general government, or of offering itself as a sacrifice, even to dismemberment, for the States beyond it.[8]

As of April 15, 1861 this matter of risking all for the sake of a principle took on new meaning, one that was not lost on the businessmen of Maryland. Lincoln's proclamation crushed political stability in the South. "The President's extraordinary proclamation" unleashed "a tornado of excitement that seems likely to sweep us all away," exclaimed Congressman Horace Maynard of Tennessee on April 18. Men who had "heretofore been cool, firm and Union loving" had become "perfectly wild" and "aroused to a phrenzy of passion."[9]

Thus, we must look at the businessmen of Baltimore City and how they chose their course on the secession issue. Baltimore City, of course, did not represent all of the business element in Maryland, but it was certainly the center of business activity in the state, and contemporary statistics show that the vast majority of trade and commerce were conducted there.[10]

Baltimore businessmen, together with other businessmen in the South, were apprehensive about the presidential election of 1860, for it represented anything but the political stability they craved. "Whatever their personal differences regarding the political situation, the Baltimore mercantile community naturally and unanimously desired to stay prosperous, and they faced the November election with the uneasy knowledge that there were uncertain times ahead for prosperity."[11] Many Baltimore businessmen were old-line Whigs and supported the Constitutional Union Party of John Bell, and the vast majority of Baltimore's merchant class were pro-South, that is voting if not for Bell then for Breckinridge. Bell and Everett's Constitutional Union Party "contained more than an appeal to late Know-Nothings and die-hard Whigs. Its platform was Southern enough to satisfy all save the most ardent proslavery advocates, enabling Baltimore merchants who had small taste for Breckinridge Democracy to vote without compromising their Southern sympathies." They also emphasized "forgetting sectional strife and keeping the Union intact, and this was precisely the sort of thing profit-minded Baltimoreans wanted to hear."[12]

Breckinridge had his supporters among Baltimore business-men, many of whom took an active part in the state convention. Many of those whose names later appeared in the group demanding a state convention and the convening of the state legislature were doubtless Breckinridge Democrats. Still, the names among the Constitutional Union supporters "would seem to indicate that a majority of the business community were loyal to the Union in November 1860, or at least to the Bell-Everett version of the Union. . . . In spite of the essential similarity of the Bell and Breckinridge platforms, each group, in Baltimore and in the South, approached the election with the strong feeling that it alone could save the Union."[13]

There is little to show that businessmen supported the Douglas Democrats in 1860. One newspaper reported that a Douglas meeting in Baltimore on November 2 was attended by some two thousand "very enthusiastic" persons, but that number considerably exceeded the forthcoming Douglas vote in the city. That meeting was organized by a handful of busi-nessmen, none of any prominence. "Old-line Baltimore Demo-crats obviously found more to their liking in the Breckinridge platform, while those who wanted compromise and an end of sectional squabbling preferred the gentle offerings of Bell; there was little room left for Douglas." The Republican Party fared worse still, despite the presence in Maryland of Montgomery Blair, who knew how to set political movements in motion.[14]

Baltimore businessmen were decidedly in favor of a Southern answer to the sectional crisis. The Baltimore *Clipper*, the leading Constitutional Unionist newspaper, denounced "black republi-

canism" with enough fervor to satisfy the most ardent secessionist, and the Bell speeches in behalf of preserving the Union were
all predicated on the assumption that Southern rights would be
secured." Despite the fist-fights and editorial sniping between
Constitutional Unionists and Southern Democrats during the
campaign—nothing out of the ordinary for an election in Baltimore—the two parties were united "on the common grounds of
distrusting Republicans and the North generally, sympathizing
with the states farther South, and seeking some means of settling
the slavery question—in favor of the South—without disrupting
the Union." When secession became a fact along the Gulf that
winter, and the chances of reaching a compromise had dimmed,
many merchants who had voted for Bell in 1860 would swing
to a more Southern point of view. "The only real difference
between Bell and Breckinridge businessmen at this time lay in
their ideas for solving the sectional disputes. . . . Few capitalists
had supported Douglas or Lincoln."[15]

As the early months of 1861 unfolded, more businessmen
swung to a stronger pro-Southern view and many of the most
prominent ones took an active part in the deliberations of the
state convention. However, with most other businessmen in the
upper South at this time, they did not take a secessionist stand.
"Coercion of the Southern states by the federal government,
with civil war in its wake, might be another question, but unless
and until it arose the general sentiment in business circles
favored staying in the Union and hoping, rather blindly, that
everything would turn out all right."[16] In March 1861 this was
the dominant sentiment throughout the upper South. Lincoln's
call for troops on April 15 forced the issue and made all decide
one way or the other.

The majority of Baltimore's businessmen were pro-South, at
least as measured by how they voted. When Lincoln issued his
call, Baltimore businessmen did not rush to volunteer to serve

or in fact support the administration in any way. Only Leopold Blumenburg, the recently immigrated German businessman who had taken up residence in Baltimore, responded along with other Germans. Baltimore businessmen did not rush forward with sums of money to support the war effort, as did businessmen in Boston, New York, Chicago, and Philadelphia. Nor did they offer goods and services to support the volunteers, as occurred in virtually every city and town north of the Mason-Dixon Line. Baltimore businessmen, in fact, responded in ways similar to most in the Upper South, with surprise, dismay, and a sense of profound disappointment in the failure of the efforts to promote peace and find compromise.

At the end of April 1861, trade and commerce were at a complete standstill in Baltimore, which spelled financial ruin for businessmen. Baltimore City and indeed the state were cut off from Virginia and the South, which meant there was no way to accomplish secession. Federal troops were only a few days or even hours away from their lightly armed and weakly fortified city, and whether Baltimore's businessmen would stand by their principles or risk losing it all was uncertain. It appears that many if not most Baltimore businessmen would have cast their lot with the South, if unthreatened and free to do so. There was simply no support for the North or the Lincoln administration's policy to use force to subjugate the South. However, when confronted with military destruction, or at the least occupation of their businesses, which would bring complete disruption of their normal business activity and thus substantial loss or even ruin, they had no choice but to acquiesce and submit to the power of federal military authorities.

By the end of May 1861, Maryland was occupied territory, and by the fall of that year the state was under firm federal control. The psychological impact of military occupations on civilian populations is beyond the scope of this work. But Virginia and the other states of the upper South did not face this immediate occupation by hostile military forces, at least not at the time when they were making the decision to secede. No one can deny the effect of having guns and cannons pointed at one's business or home, creating the imminent prospect of financial ruin. To illustrate, we will look at the impact this military occupation had on one of Maryland's most well-known businesses and its equally well-known president—the Baltimore and Ohio Railroad and John W. Garrett.

The B&O had an important role in Maryland's secession spring, and perhaps no other single business had as much impact on settling the issue for Maryland as did the B&O. For it was this railroad that connected the North with Washington, and it was this road that General Scott had to control at all cost, without regard to Maryland's economic welfare. "The Washington Branch was the last link in the chain of railroad communication between the North and the National Capital. It was also the only way by rail."[17] In addition, although three-fourths of the Baltimore and Ohio Railroad lay on Virginia soil, it was a Maryland business through and through. The State of Maryland and the City of Baltimore had invested heavily in its securities, and in their corporate capacities had come to its relief on more than one occasion. Both civic entities had driven hard bargains in the public interest, and they counted a majority of six on its board of directors. The state took one-fifth of the gross passenger receipts of the Washington Branch under the guise of a capitation tax. Practically all of the stock was held by the city, the state, or Maryland residents. "There was substance indeed in the current claim that the Baltimore and Ohio was a Maryland enterprise."[18]

Its president, John Work Garrett, was a pro-Southern Marylander and considered his railroad a Southern line. That much seemed evident in his actions until late 1860. Garrett had been greatly disturbed by John Brown's Raid on Harper's Ferry in

1859, and he had immediately offered the B&O's services to authorities in Washington and Richmond in putting down the insurrection. That attitude dovetailed with the sympathies of the B&O's board of directors, which was dominated by proslavery men. Nevertheless, "it can hardly be doubted that his action was sincere and his sentiments the product of his Southern background."[19] In a speech at Baltimore, Garrett left no doubt about where he and his railroad would come down in a sectional conflict.

> It is a Southern Line. And if ever necessity require—which heaven forbid!—it will prove the great bulwark of the border, and a sure agency for home defense. It has the ability, sir, with its equipment of 4,000 locomotives and cars, to transport daily 10,000 troops and with its disciplined force of 3,500 men has always in service the nucleus of an army. During a period when agitation, alarm and uncertainty prevail, is it not right, is it not becoming, that Baltimore should declare her position in "the irrepressible conflict" threatened and urged by Northern fanaticism?[20]

But by early 1861 the B&O had begun to lose business as Western shippers started sending their goods by more northerly routes, partly in response to Maryland's pro-Southern stand and partly out of fear of secessionist disruptions. Garrett's public appearance became more moderate, and he became much less visible. His "effervescence" was soon supplanted by "studied decision . . . for the heart soon gave way to the head."[21] After all, Garrett was a businessman whose principal role was to make money for his railroad.

The problems facing his road were substantial and in a matter of a few short weeks became overwhelming. In February, President-elect Lincoln refused to use the B&O on his journey from Springfield to Washington in favor of more northerly roads. In April, when Lincoln called for troops, Garrett's own friends—his

Marylanders—threatened him personally and tore up his tracks. Both Secretary of War Cameron (the former president of the Northern Central and a hated competitor) and Governor Letcher of Virginia threatened confiscation of his railroad, or at least the portions they controlled, if he did not cede to their demands. In addition, the Northern press attacked him and the B&O for supposedly secessionist activities. Garrett was indeed in a dilemma. His fellow Marylanders insisted that the B&O not be used to aid the Lincoln administration, and his arch-enemy, Simon Cameron, was trying to take over his railroad for government use. "[Garrett] asked the War Department for safe conduct for his regular trains only to find officialdom obstinate. He was curtly informed that the entire capacity of the military railway was needed for troop movements."[22]

In fact, things did get worst for Garrett. At Harper's Ferry, Confederates under General Thomas J. "Stonewall" Jackson commandeered a large portion of his rolling stock, and the federal army took over most of his line. By January 1862, Congress had passed a bill placing railroads under the control of the government, and the secretary of war placed the B&O under War Department control on May 25, 1862. Garrett acceded to the government's wishes but "with the tacit understanding that the road would be permitted to operate as a private line so long as it satisfactorily met the demands of the government."[23]

Thus confronted, Garrett made his peace with the Lincoln administration—he made a business decision to save his railroad by acquiescing to the dictates of the federal government. By agreeing to play the game, he was permitted "to operate as a private line" provided he "satisfactorily met the demands of the government." Here then, was a businessman doing what he had to do keep his business alive. In so doing he saved not only his railroad but the investments of hundreds of Marylanders who held securities in it. Festus P. Summers summarized the importance of the B&O to Maryland in the secession crisis this way:

> The value of the road, however, did not stem altogether from
> the forty miles of inanimate iron that connected Baltimore
> and Washington. Because of its unique geographical location
> and of its fiscal and administrative dependence upon Mary-
> land and Baltimore, it was strategically situated to turn the
> course of public opinion in that pro-Southern city and to
> shape public policy in the state at large. Because it kept trains
> moving and always acted the passive role of an endangered
> public work, the company was not without influence in the
> pacification of Maryland.[24]

Superb military strategist that he was, Winfield Scott knew
that control of the B&O was a military imperative, for it was the
only railroad between Washington and Baltimore, and Baltimore was where all railroads from the North and West connected. Scott's order to have federal troops quickly seize and
hold the line of the B&O put the Maryland business community
on notice concerning just what they could expect if they opposed the government. This had a significant effect on settling
the issue of secession in Maryland because it neutralized the
state's secession-leaning business community. A clear majority
of Maryland's business community was pro-South and would
have opted to join the South if permitted to do so in the spring
of 1861. As federal regiments occupied the state, many businessmen chose to make accommodation with the occupiers rather
than close down their businesses and lose all. The winter of
1860–1861 was indeed bleak for Baltimore businesses.

> During this period the trade of Baltimore and a large part of
> the state had suffered a great falling off in volume. The
> military authorities had placed an embargo upon the com-
> merce of Baltimore. Consequently goods were shipped to and
> from more fortunate centers. . . . Later the city of Baltimore
> began to profit by war contracts and war business; but not to

the extent of her Northern rivals, whose trade and manufacturing began to grow by leaps and bounds.[25]

During the secession winter, no one foresaw the long and
incredibly destructive war that was about to unfold. And as it
turned out, Baltimore and its mercantile class were spared the
devastation experienced by many other Southern cities.

8

Conclusion

I hear the distant thunder hum, Maryland!
The Old Line bugle, fife, and drum, Maryland!
She is not dead, nor deaf, nor dumb—
Huzza! she spurns the Northern scum!
She breathes—she burns! she'll come! she'll come!
Maryland! My Maryland!

James Ryder Randall

J Thomas Scharf, whose history of Maryland is regarded as one of the best works of its kind, observed, ". . . from the beginning of the Republic, Maryland aligned itself with the Southern States."[1] Most agree that this was the case. Of the original thirteen states, six were regarded as Southern—Delaware, Maryland, Virginia, North Carolina, South Carolina, and Georgia—and seven as Northern—Massachusetts, New Hampshire, Rhode Island, Connecticut, New York, New Jersey, and Pennsylvania.

And, in the great sectional controversies of the early years of the republic, Maryland almost always sided with the South. In 1787, when one of the first great sectional issues was voted upon—whether the navigation rights to the Mississippi River should be ceded to Spain—Maryland cast her lot with the South. In 1821 another great sectional issue, whether Missouri should be admitted to the Union as a slave state, came before the House of Representatives and, again, Maryland cast her lot with the South. Maryland's representatives unanimously voted in favor of admission while some of her sister states' delegations were divided: Virginia voted eighteen to two in favor, and North Carolina voted nine to two in favor.[2] At one of the last great Southern commercial conventions in the late 1850s, when the issue of restricting the slave trade was voted upon, Maryland cast all of her votes with the lower South, voting against restrictions and supporting the continuance of the slave trade. As mentioned in the previous chapter, these conventions "were held partly to foster sectional unity on important commercial issues, and Maryland played a leading role in most of these efforts. They represented a determined challenge on the part of Southern businessmen to check the Northern dominance of the nation's commerce and trade."[3]

Although there was great diversity of opinion in the nation during 1860 and the early months of 1861, when the call to war came on April 15, the sections were all but united diametrically opposed to one another. The North responded to Lincoln's call for troops overwhelmingly; the South turned away. This sectionalism is all-important to our conclusion regarding the secession of Maryland, for the secession movement turned out to be just that—a sectional issue. No state in the North seriously considered secession while every state in the South did. Numerous historians have examined the sectional crisis and discussed it in great detail. Those close to it felt its tragedy. In 1896 Edward Ingle wrote almost wistfully of how nearly it might have been avoided.

> In one respect it was unfortunate for this country that the great highways of transportation and travel should have been extended more rapidly from east to west than from north to south. . . . though Southerners and Northerners came into

close personal contact beyond the Alleghanies, their intercourse did not develop before 1860 sufficient power to affect
favorably for harmony the two original sections of the seaboard. The inhabitants of these had, before the age of the
railroad and the telegraph, comparatively few opportunities
to learn to know each other, and afterward their trend of
travel was on parallel lines instead of on intersecting ones.
Their politicians met at Washington. But that city was the
great hustings of the country; and sentiments expressed there
were too frequently designed to maintain a man's popularity
in his own section, rather than to cultivate friendly relations
among all parts of the country. . . . There were, in fact, few
factors in the expansion of the United States working toward
the destruction of sectionalism, that had existed before the
Constitution.[4]

By the 1850s the sections were truly at odds. At odds, to be
sure over slavery, but at odds over a host of other issues as well,
and each one touched some particular part of the populace. For
instance, the tariff policy that protected Northern manufacturing simply outraged Southern agricultural interests, because it
cost them more to buy their goods with a tariff placed on cheaper
foreign imports. Yet another example was the federal government's policy for expending funds on internal improvements,
such as railroads and highways—almost all monies were spent
in the North, which outraged Southerners and especially the
mercantile class. Some have argued that this was the single most
important factor in bringing the sections to war. And, indeed,
the South was right—they were not getting their fair share of
funds for internal improvements. During this era, the South
watched the North steadily increase its representation in Congress and its control over the government and thereby over the
nation's purse strings. In the end, what drove the sections apart
was the dynamic struggle over those most fundamental human
treasures: money and power.

This sectional tug-of-war, then, put the men of the South, and especially the men of the upper South, in a terrible quandary. Many, if not most, Southerners were moderates who preferred to see sectional differences worked out in some reasonable way, as they had been in the past. But this reasonable way had to make some accommodation to the Southern viewpoint. When no accommodation was forthcoming, these men had to make a choice, and the majority chose to stay with their section, which meant to support the secession of the Southern states. Avery Craven concluded:

> There were far more Southerners who loved the nation and gloried in its achievements but who saw their section losing its comparative strength, felt the sting of Northern charges, true and false, and feared the growing tendency to make slavery and its restriction the basis for denying their section an equality or a chance for equality in national life. . . . This great body of Southerners gradually accepted secession as the only way out. Seemingly the radical element in the North was gaining control. . . . The Republican party was gaining strength. The spirit of tolerance and co-operation was ending. It was a case of submission or secession, and they made their choice. . . . The pressure of public opinion, the loss of hope because of the actions of Northern conservatives, the growing stubbornness and open hostility of increasing numbers at the North, the breakup of the Democratic party and Lincoln's election—these things forced conservative men to choose between the North, which was seemingly indifferent, and the South, of which they were a part in many ways. They made their choice in sorrow that easily turned to bitterness and hatred. They understood it to be a case of "fighting or running."[5]

This sectional play on the attitudes of the men and women of the day must not be underestimated. In the end, they would stick with their roots, with their locales, and with their states.

Frederick Jackson Turner commented:

> Men are not absolutely dictated to by climate, geography, soils, or economic interests. The influence of the stock from which they sprang, the inherited ideals, the spiritual factors, often triumph over material interests. There is also the influence of personality. Men do follow leaders, and sometimes into paths inconsistent with the section's material interests. But in the long run the statesman must speak the language of his people on fundamentals, both of interests and ideals.[6]

"But in the long run the statesman must speak the language of his people on the fundamentals, both of interests and ideals." The leaders of Maryland did speak the language of their people—they spoke with outrage at the actions of the Lincoln administration in the spring and summer of 1861 and continued to do so until they were arrested or compelled to leave the state. And the majority of Marylanders were true to their section and their state. They supported the South and opposed the North until the overwhelming force of the federal military forced them to cease free and open expression.

Certainly, a strong case can be made that Maryland was a Southern state. She consistently acted in concert with the South from the earliest days of the republic. And in the crucial presidential election of 1860, she voted very much like the Southern states of the upper South. The evidence supports the notion that in the spring of 1861 Maryland would have seceded and joined her "section," the South. In review:

As a region, the South was diverse in its opinions and divided on the secession issue. In virtually every Southern state, Southerners were divided by geography, by economic status, and by social background. They were divided on the matter of secession. The lack of cohesion or concerted action in the South on the question of secession during the winter of 1861 was probably due to the fact that most people believed that some compromise would be worked out to save the Union. This lack of action on secession, however, had a profound impact on the secession movement in Maryland, for it delayed the drive toward secession in the state.

In "The Election," the votes cast in the presidential election of 1860 were examined from the context of looking for similar voting patterns in the sections, North *vs.* South. And, indeed there were patterns, the central one being that the election was overwhelmingly sectional. Almost all Northerners voted for one of the two parties of the North, and conversely, almost all Southerners voted for one of the two parties of the South. And Maryland voted identically to the upper South that seceded. She gave 91 percent of her vote to the candidates of the Southern parties, only 9 percent to the Northern ones, and virtually no support to the extremist Northern candidate, Abraham Lincoln. The extremist Southern candidate and the moderate Southern candidate ran equally well throughout the state. Many of the slaveholding oligarchy voted for the moderate, Bell, while many non-slaveholders voted for the extremist, Breckinridge. Thus, in what turned out to be the last free expression of opinion in the state for some five years, Marylanders voted with their section and matched, or looked very similar to, any of the states of the upper South that seceded. Conversely, Marylanders rejected Northern parties overwhelmingly. The Mason-Dixon Line looked very real when Lincoln carried Pennsylvania with 56 percent of its vote, while Maryland gave him only 2.5 percent of hers. Of course, the presidential election of 1860 was not run on the issue of secession, although the Southern Democrats threatened to do just that if Lincoln were elected. However, the election results illustrate that the presidential election of 1860 was a sectional election and Maryland voted unquestionably as a Southern state.

Chapter 3, "The State" illustrated how the secessionists of Maryland were tied to the Virginians. Marylanders were simply unwilling to act until Virginia made her choice. As it played out, Virginia's vote to secede came after Lincoln's Proclamation of Insurrection, which along with the attack on Fort Sumter spurred the North to mobilize for war. Maryland was overrun by Northern troops (on their way to save the nation's capital) before she could act on secession.

Chapter 4, "The Month," provided a day-by-day account of April's crucial events as they likely would have been viewed by the secessionists of Maryland. Prior to the fifteenth of April, Maryland reacted similarly to the rest of the upper South—her citizens urged compromise and hoped for the best. Indeed, most Marylanders, at that time, favored staying in the Union provided the Union made some accommodation with the South. In the event that was not forthcoming, many of Maryland's leading citizens were prepared to act with Virginia. They stayed closely aligned with that state throughout this uncertain period. As a practical matter, Maryland could not have seceded without Virginia seceding first.

Most Marylanders, like most Southerners, were firmly opposed to the federal government's coercing any Southern state to remain in the Union. In fact, a great many Americans of the day felt that states did have a right to secede from the Union. Even abolitionist-prone Massachusetts had threatened to secede in earlier years of the Republic.

After April 15, the day of Lincoln's Proclamation of Insurrection and his call for troops to put it down, Maryland again resembled the upper South. Stunned and outraged, Marylanders refused to answer the call for troops. They rose as one to stop what Southerners considered Northern aggression. Blood was shed in Baltimore. The authorities summoned the Maryland militia; efforts were made to prevent Northern troops from crossing the state. And the

Lincoln administration moved quickly to occupy Maryland militarily, urged on by the fiery Northern press.

What must have stunned each and every Marylander was the magnitude and rapidity of the Northern response to Lincoln's call for troops. Northern states responded with not thousands but tens of thousands of volunteers, with huge sums of money, and with men appearing at Northern armories overnight. The Southern Confederacy's firing on Fort Sumter galvanized the North, just as Lincoln's call for troops electrified the South. Northern troops, at least most of them, were quickly put in motion toward Washington, and thereby Maryland. By the last week in April Marylanders were bombarded by calls from an incredibly hostile Northern press for the military occupation of their state. These same papers reported thousands of Northern troops massed on Maryland's border and some already in the state.

General Winfield Scott was a superb military strategist who moved as quickly and adroitly as he could to isolate Maryland from the South. He moved to secure and control her railroads and highways. He moved to control the Chesapeake and the Potomac and the strategically important Fort Monroe at the mouth of the Chesapeake Bay. And he moved to occupy key cities and towns in the state—first the towns of Perryville and Havre de Grace, then Annapolis and Relay, and finally Baltimore, Frederick, and Cumberland. In the end, what closed the door on Maryland's secessionists was the speed with which federal regiments occupied the state. A mere ten days after the citizens of Baltimore fought Northern troops in the streets, Maryland was overrun by thousands of armed Northern soldiers.

Finally, chapter 4 attempted to examine the events of April from the perspective of Maryland's secessionists. It seems clear that the Lincoln administration early on planned for the military occupation of Maryland. General Scott unleashed his Little

Anaconda Plan as soon as he felt prepared to do so. Lincoln responded to the urgings of the Northern press and indeed most of the people of the North when he ordered federal troops to occupy the state, irrespective of the law or the Constitution. The Lincoln administration was absolutely determined to preserve the federal capital at Washington, and if that meant Maryland had to be occupied by military force and her people subjugated, so be it. From the federal government's perspective, Maryland was a small state with neither great wealth nor large population and, thus, could be sacrificed for preserving the capital.

Chapter 5, "The End," highlighted events of the summer and fall of 1861 to illustrate how the federal military systematically destroyed the secession movement in Maryland. First, the army occupied the cities and towns of the state. Second, they suspended the writ of habeas corpus, thereby placing federal military authority over that of the Constitution and its agents, the federal and state courts. Third, they arbitrarily arrested and imprisoned prominent leaders of the state, including most of the important elected political officials (most of whom were secessionist). Fourth, they suppressed the free press of the state (most of which was pro-South). Finally, they assisted in rigging an election in the state whereby a governor and legislature were elected to carry out the wishes of the Lincoln administration. During this time—roughly mid-April to early November 1861—the Lincoln administration simply treated Maryland as if she had seceded.

The federal military forced Maryland to stay in the Union. The Lincoln administration knew that the federal capital had to remain in Washington for practical reasons and for psychological ones. The machinery of the federal government realistically could not be moved, and equally important, Washington represented the unity of the nation. To move it would have been an admission of disunion.

Although a minority of people in Maryland genuinely supported the North, many of these were in fact new residents; that is, they were born out of the state or were descendants of Northerners who had recently immigrated to the northern and western parts of the state.

The evidence suggests that, if free to choose, Marylanders would have opted to join the Southern Confederacy, thereby staying with their section. A sizeable majority of Marylanders, it appears, always and consistently supported the South. And conversely, they truly rejected Northern political ideas.

In the end, the citizens of the state would have chosen: a Southern star for Maryland.

Postscript

After the war, Maryland rather quickly returned to normal. The old-line families and the names familiar to Marylanders began to re-appear and assume leading roles in politics and business. As before the war, they were a pro-Southern group. The Marylanders who had gone South began to come home in large numbers—William Wilkens Glenn reported that as early as June 29, 1865, some 11,700 paroled Marylanders had already registered at the provost-marshal's office in Baltimore alone.[7] The War of the Rebellion, as it is referred to in the *Official Records,* was officially declared over by President Johnson on April 2, 1866. And at about this time, conservative Unionists and the old Democrats united to throw out the oppressive war politicians. The result was that the state returned to the pro- Southern political stance it had shown before the war. In fact, the Democrats regained control of the State House in 1869 and retained control until 1896. A review of the list of Democratic governors of this era finds many old Maryland names:

Governor Oden Bowie, 1869–72
Governor William Pinkney Whyte, 1872–74
Governor James Black Groome, 1874–76
Governor John L. Carroll, 1876–80
Governor William T. Hamilton, 1880–84
Governor Robert M. McLane, 1884–85
Governor Henry Lloyd, 1885–88
Governor Elihu Emory, 1888–92
Governor Frank Brown, 1892–96.

At the end of the war, Maryland's radical Unionist leaders—Western Maryland's Francis Thomas and Baltimore's Henry Winter Davis—were still in league with the Radical Republicans in Washington and did everything in their power to oppose the new coalition. In fact Thomas, who at the time was a member of the Maryland congressional delegation, declared on the floor of the House of Representatives that Maryland was falling into the hands of the disloyal element again and urged the federal government to intervene. But by 1867, as noted above, Marylanders had elected a pro-Southern governor, Oden Bowie, son of the old Maryland Bowies. In addition, they adopted a new pro-Southern constitution (pro-Southern because it permitted those returning from the South to participate immediately in state politics); and, in general, they regained control of the political and business apparatus of the state. This was a fascinating period in Maryland's history, and the interested reader is referred to Scharf's *History of Maryland* and to William Starr Myers' work, *The Self-Reconstruction of Maryland, 1864–1867*.

This postscript highlights some of the more noteworthy occurrences in Maryland after the war and after the old guard returned, which illustrate Maryland's pro-Southern nature. Of course, none of this can be directly linked to the secession movement, but it demonstrates how many Marylanders felt toward the South. In no particular order of importance, here were some of the ways Marylanders expressed themselves after the war.

—Maryland was the only state outside of the original Confederacy to establish a Confederate Soldiers Home supported by state appropriations.

—For the next half century, the political leaders of Maryland appointed to the adjutant general post—the head of the Maryland Guard and the ranking military officer in the state—mainly men who had served the South. The list of these distinguished Marylanders:

MG George H. Bier, CSA	1869–1871
MG Charles H. McBlair, CSA	1871–1874
MG Frank A. Bond, CSA	1874–1880
MG J. Wesley Watkins, USA	1880–1884
MG James Howard, CSA	1884–1892
MG Henry Kyd Douglas, CSA	1892–1896
MG L. Allison Wilmer, USA	1896–1900
MG John S. Saunders, CSA	1900–1904

—Marylanders did not recognize the Union men in their midst, at least not like Northern states did. In fact, it was not until 1896, more than three decades after the close of the war, that Maryland compiled a list of its GAR men and their regiments. It was published as the *History and Roster of Maryland Volunteers*. These searching words from its preface told the story:

> The survivors of the Civil War and their descendants in the State of Maryland had, for years, hoped that the example set by the other States of the Union, in the compilation and publication of the records of their heroic sons, would have been an incentive to the people of our State to do likewise, as the record of the gallantry of a part of our people would be the common heritage of all. Over three decades had passed—in fact, a third of a century had rolled on since the close of the greatest civil war history has recorded, and the archives of the State failed to show the muster rolls of her sons, or even a brief record of their splendid achievements.[8]

—After the war, Northern states honored their Union war heroes—not so in Maryland. There would be no honoring Thomas Holiday Hicks.

Yet another example of the true Maryland can be found in the names of those who stood up to be counted for the South. At the time of his arrest in September 1861, Francis Key Howard had among his papers a list of Baltimoreans who had declared themselves in favor of the South and in favor of Maryland's secession. More than 250 names appeared on the list, and they were noteworthy. A careful examination showed that they represented practically every old-line family of the city.[9]

Another expression of sentiment in the state is evident in how Marylanders voted after the war. Three crucial elections illustrate the point: first, the election for or against a new state constitution in September 1867; second, the gubernatorial election of November 1867; and third, the presidential election of 1868.

Maryland was forced to adopt a new constitution in 1864 that was largely the work of the state's radical Unionists aided and abetted by the Lincoln administration and the federal army. This so-called constitution was extreme, restrictive, and disliked by most Marylanders. Early in 1867 a commission of distinguished Marylanders was appointed to draft a new state constitution to replace the one forced on the populace in 1864. The Constitution of 1867 re-established representative government in the state and was decidedly pro-Southern, for it eliminated all of the barriers to free and open elections, which, as previously mentioned, opened the doors of political power to Marylanders returning from the South as well as former Democrats who essentially had been disenfranchised by the Constitution of 1864. The radical Unionists were wholeheartedly against this new constitution and campaigned vigorously for its defeat. In a stunning rejection of the radical Unionists, Marylanders voted for the new constitution by more than two to one: 47,152 to 23,036.

Shortly after the vote on the new constitution, the gubernatorial election was held in which the pro-Southern candidate, Oden Bowie, Democratic conservative, ran against Judge Hugh Lenox Bond, radical Unionist. In an even more lop-sided victory, Bowie beat Bond by 63,694 to 22,050. Scharf commented: "The conservatives [Democratic conservatives], knowing their heavy preponderance, did not poll by any means their full strength, yet they elected all their state officers and carried both branches of the legislature, a fact unprecedented in the history of the State."[10]

Finally, the presidential election of 1868 pitted Republican war hero General Ulysses S. Grant against Democrat Horatio Seymour. Marylanders overwhelmingly rejected Grant and the Republicans, voting for Seymour, 62,365 to 30,442. According to John T. Willis:

> On election day the Democrats carried every county and Baltimore City in rolling up an impressive margin of better than two to one. . . . Like a tightly wrapped coil, the Maryland voters, once unleashed, gave a strong repudiation to the Federal domination of Maryland during the war and the post-war policies of a Republican reconstruction Congress. For Maryland, a new era in presidential politics had begun.[11]

Marylanders in fact would not give a majority to a Republican presidential candidate for forty years.

How did Marylanders vote when free to express themselves? By 1867 the military was no longer present, loyalty oaths were no longer required, and intimidation and coercion at polling places were gone. The results indicate a remarkably consistent voting pattern, in which roughly two-thirds of Marylanders voted along pro-Southern lines, and about one-third voted along unconditional Union lines. Of course, it would be an unwarranted stretch of logic to conclude that all of this pro-

Election	Democrat (pro-Southern)	Republican (radical Union)
Constitution of 1867	47,152 (67%)	23,036 (33%)
Gubernatorial 1867	63,694 (74%)	22,050 (26%)
Presidential 1868	62,365 (67%)	30,442 (33%)

Southern vote would have opted for secession in 1861 or that all of the radical Union vote would have supported Lincoln unconditionally. In fact, these data *prove* nothing, yet they do give some sense of the true sentiment of Marylanders relative to the South. Certainly it was true that part of this two-thirds majority were Unionists during the war. But with the federal military constantly present around their homes and businesses; with their traditional leaders mostly in the South or imprisoned; and subject to the spying of unconditional Unionists who might at any time run to the federal military with some tale of disloyal behavior—it must have been equally true that much of this Unionism was either coerced or simply expedient behavior. What seems clear though, is that when free to vote as they chose, Marylanders rejected the Republicans by substantial majorities, just as they had done before the war.

Perhaps the most significant of all indications of Maryland's true sentiment relative to secession can be found in the incredible financial support Marylanders gave to the South after the war. The leading men of Maryland immediately sprang to the South's relief.

The intense sympathy felt in Maryland for the sufferings of the Southern people soon found active expression in devoted charitable deeds. Shortly after the close of the war, in 1865, a number of Baltimore gentlemen, irrespective of party, organized an agricultural aid society to supply a portion of the Southern states, and more particularly Virginia, with stock, farming tools, and seed. For this purpose, over eighty thousand dollars were subscribed and judiciously distributed.[13]

Significant monies were raised by the women of Baltimore, who in April 1866 organized a fair and collected a staggering sum of over $164,569.94, largely in small donations from middle-class people, for the Southern Relief effort. The average Baltimorean responded to this call in a very substantial way. The money was distributed to Virginia ($27,000), North Carolina ($16,500), South Carolina ($19,750), Georgia ($17,875), Alabama ($16,250), Mississippi ($20,625), Louisiana ($7,500), Florida ($5,500), Arkansas ($5,000), Tennessee ($12,500), Maryland refugees ($10,000), and miscellaneous donations ($6,069.94).[14]

These fairs and other relief efforts continued for many years. The Maryland legislature also came to the aid of the South, appropriating some $100,000 in 1867 alone. These were substantial sums in 1867. They undoubtedly represented deep and true sentiments on the part of the people of Maryland.

What can be drawn from this evidence? Simply this: Marylanders consistently expressed Southern sentiment. They voted in patterns similar to their Southern counterparts before the war, and after the war they did so again. Marylanders, as a whole, rejected the North with the same fervor as all Southerners. After the war, Marylanders honored their sons who had served the South, many of whom assumed roles of leadership and stature. It is axiomatic that Maryland did not secede, but the final point to repeat is this: from April 1861, to the very end of the war, Lincoln and his administration treated Maryland as if she had seceded.

What we shall some day become will grow inexorably out of what we are; and what we are now, in its turn, comes out of what earlier Americans were—out of what they did and thought and dreamed and hoped for, out of their trials and their aspirations, out of their shining victories and their dark and tragic defeats.

Bruce Catton

NOTES

Introduction

1. Bruce Catton, *Reflections on the Civil War* (New York: Berkley Books, 1982), 26.
2. Ibid., 33.

Chapter 1: Setting the Stage

1. Jesse T. Carpenter, *The South as a Conscious Minority* (New York: New York University Press, 1930), 22–23.
2. George L. P. Radcliffe, *Governor Thomas H. Hicks of Maryland and the Civil War* (Baltimore: The Johns Hopkins University Press, 1901), preface.
3. Avery O. Craven, *The Growth of Southern Nationalism, 1848–1861* (Baton Rouge: Louisiana State University Press, 1953), 7–9.
4. Ibid.
5. Georgia Lee Tatum, *Disloyalty in the Confederacy* (Chapel Hill: University of North Carolina Press, 1934), 4.
6. Ibid., 12.
7. James G. Randall and David Donald, *The Civil War and Reconstruction* (Boston: D. C. Heath and Company, 1961), 138.
8. Tatum, *Disloyalty in the Confederacy*, 6–7.
9. Randall and Donald, *The Civil War and Reconstruction*, 137–38.
10. Tatum, *Disloyalty in the Confederacy*, 9–10.
11. Randall and Donald, *Civil War and Reconstruction*, 141.
12. Ibid.
13. Tatum, *Disloyalty in the Confederacy*, 11–12.
14. Randall and Donald, *Civil War and Reconstruction*, 181.
15. Tatum, *Disloyalty in the Confederacy*, 5.
16. Randall and Donald, *Civil War and Reconstruction*, 183.
17. Tatum, *Disloyalty in the Confederacy*, 8–9.
18. Randall and Donald, *Civil War and Reconstruction*, 185–86.
19. Tatum, *Disloyalty in the Confederacy*, 5–6.
20. Randall and Donald, *Civil War and Reconstruction*, 186–87.
21. Tatum, *Disloyalty in the Confederacy*, 10.
22. Ibid., 4.
23. Randall and Donald, *Civil War and Reconstruction*, 188.
24. Richard Walsh and William Lloyd Fox, *Maryland, A History,*

25. Charles C. Anderson, *Fighting by Southern Federals* (New York: The Neale Publishing Company, 1912), 10–13.

26. Jean Harvey Baker, *The Politics of Continuity* (Baltimore: The Johns Hopkins University Press, 1973), 2–3.

27. Ibid., 3–4.

28. Matthew Page Andrews, *History of Maryland: Province and State* (Hatboro, Md.: Tradition Press, 1965), 475–79.

29. Ibid., 482–83.

30. Radcliffe, *Governor Thomas H. Hicks*, 15.

Chapter 2: The Election

1. Daniel W. Crofts, *Reluctant Confederates* (Chapel Hill: University of North Carolina Press, 1989), 54.

2. Edward C. Smith, *The Borderland in the Civil War* (Freeport, 1927, repr. Books for Libraries Press, 1969) 49–50.

3. Baker, *Politics of Continuity,* 42–43.

4. Dwight L. Dumond, *The Secession Movement, 1860–1861* (New York: The MacMillan Company, 1931), 2–3.

5. Craven, *Growth of Southern Nationalism,* 334–35.

6. Smith, *The Borderland in the Civil War,* 52.

7. Dumond, *The Secession Movement,* 96–99.

8. Craven, *Growth of Southern Nationalism,* 339.

9. Ollinger Crenshaw, *The Slave States in the Presidential Election of 1860* (Baltimore: The Johns Hopkins University Press, 1945), 60.

10. Cited in Baker, *Politics of Continuity,* 39–40.

11. Craven, *Growth of Southern Nationalism,* 336–37.

12. Dumond, *The Secession Movement,* 93.

13. Ibid., 94.

14. Arthur M. Schlesinger, Jr., and Fred L. Israel, *History of American Presidential Elections, 1789–1968* (New York: Chelsea House Publishers, 1971), 1152.

15. J. Thomas Scharf, *History of Maryland* (repr.; Hatboro, Md.: Tradition Press, 1967), 356–58.

16. Ibid., 354–55.

17. Dumond, *The Secession Movement,* 93.

18. Crofts, *Reluctant Confederates,* 193.

19. David Y. Thomas, "Southern Non-Slaveholders in the Election of 1860," *Political Science Quarterly,* 26 (1911): 222–34; Crofts, *Reluctant Confederates.*

20. Thomas, "Southern Non-Slaveholders," 222–34.

21. Ibid., 226–27.

22. Crofts, *Reluctant Confederates*, 45.

23. Ibid., 67–81.

24. Darrell W. Overdyke, *The Know-Nothing Party in the South* (Binghamton, N.Y.: Vail-Ballou Press, 1950), 49.

25. Baker, *Politics of Continuity*, 25.

26. Ibid., 28.

27. Smith, *The Borderland in the Civil War*, 61.

28. Dumond, *The Secession Movement*, 108–9.

29. Crofts, *Reluctant Confederates*, 258.

30. E. B. Long, *The Civil War Day by Day* (New York: Da Capo Press, Inc., 1971), 65.

Chapter 3: The State

1. Crofts, *Reluctant Confederates*, 136.

2. William C. Wright, *The Secession Movement in the Middle Atlantic States* (Rutherford, N.J.: Fairleigh Dickinson University Press, 1973), 27.

3. Charles Branch Clark, *The Eastern Shore of Maryland and Virginia* (New York: Lewis Historical Publishing Co., 1950), 542.

4. November 27, 1860.

5. Smith, *The Borderland in the Civil War*, 139.

6. Radcliffe, *Governor Thomas H. Hicks*, 80.

7. Smith, *The Borderland in the Civil War*, 86.

8. Crofts, *Reluctant Confederates*, 195.

9. Ibid., 199.

10. Dumond, *The Secession Movement, 1860–1861*, 244–45.

11. Crofts, *Reluctant Confederates*, 138.

12. Ibid., 139.

13. Randall and Donald, *The Civil War and Reconstruction*, 152.

14. *Baltimore Sun*, February 20, 1861.

15. *Baltimore Clipper*, February 19, 1861.

16. Radcliffe, *Governor Thomas H. Hicks*, 42.

17. Smith, *The Borderland in the Civil War*, 109.

18. Ibid., 156.

19. Ibid., 110.

20. For the reader interested in the change of Virginia's vote on secession, a noteworthy source can be found in the letters of E. C. Burk, a member of the Virginia legislature in 1860–1861, in J. E. Walmsley,

"The Change of Secession Sentiment in Virginia in 1861," *American Historical Review*, 31 (1925): 180–219.

Chapter 4: The Month

1. The press in Maryland and in the North not only reported in great detail on the happenings but through their editorials portrayed the views of their respective sections. Two newspapers will be quoted extensively in this chapter, the *Baltimore Sun* and the *New York Times*. The *Sun* was regarded as a moderate newspaper of the day and presented a balanced, less partisan point of view—in fact it was one of only a handful of newspapers that the federal military authorities permitted to operate after the occupation of Baltimore. The *New York Times* also took a relatively moderate position and was regarded as a reliable newspaper of the time.
2. Radcliffe, *Governor Thomas H. Hicks,* 16–17.
3. *Baltimore Sun*, April 5, 1861.
4. Crofts, *Reluctant Confederates,* 233–34.
5. The source for the daily activities is E. B. Long's, *The Civil War Day by Day.*
6. Crofts, *Reluctant Confederates,* 307.
7. *Official Records,* ser. 4, 1:151.
8. George William Brown, *Baltimore and the 19th of April, 1861* (1887. repr. Baltimore: Maclay & Associates, 1982), 30.
9. Bayly Ellen Marks and Mark Norton Schatz, eds., *Between North and South—A Maryland Journalist Views the Civil War: The Narrative of William Wilkens Glenn, 1861–1869* (Rutherford, N.J.: Fairleigh Dickinson University Press, 1976), 25.
10. Crofts, *Reluctant Confederates,* 308.
11. Ibid., 295.
12. Radcliffe, *Governor Thomas H. Hicks,* 67.
13. Scharf, *History of Maryland,* 363.
14. Marks and Schatz, eds., *Between North and South,* 21.
15. Randall and Donald, *Civil War and Reconstruction,* 182.
16. *Official Records,* ser. 1, 2:581.
17. Radcliffe, *Governor Thomas H. Hicks,* 51.
18. Brown, *Baltimore and the 19th of April,* 34.
19. Scharf, *History of Maryland,* 400.
20. Randall and Donald summarized this way. "Throughout the whole

situation one sees the unfortunate effect of Lincoln's April policy. Feeling that Lincoln should have given conciliation a better trial, that he should above all have avoided a crisis at Sumter, conservative Southerners were deeply outraged at what they deemed both a stroke of bad policy and a breaking of administration promises. As for his call for troops, it served in one flash to alienate that whole mass of Union sentiment which, while not pro-Lincoln, was nevertheless antisecessionist and constituted Lincoln's best chance of saving the Union without war." *The Civil War and Reconstruction,* 188–89.

21. Crofts, *Reluctant Confederates,* 313.
22. Radcliffe, *Governor Thomas H. Hicks,* 52.
23. Ibid., 46.
24. *Official Records,* ser. 1, 2:578.
25. Ibid., ser. 1, 2:579.
26. Scharf, *History of Maryland,* 400.
27. The best account of the riot is George William Brown, *Baltimore and the 19th of April.*
28. *Official Records,* ser. 1, 2:578.
29. Bruce Catton, *Reflections on the Civil War,* 26–27.
30. Brown, *Baltimore and the 19th of April,* 26.
31. *Baltimore Sun,* April 20, 1861.
32. Radcliffe, *Governor Thomas H. Hicks,* 59.
33. *Official Records,* ser. 1, 2:583.
34. Ibid., ser. 1, 2:587.
35. Marks and Schatz, eds., *Between North and South,* 83.
36. Paul M. Angle and Earl Schenck Miers, *The Tragic years, 1860–1865* (New York: Simon and Schuster, 1960), 81.
37. *Official Records,* ser. 1, 2:585.
38. Ibid., ser. 1, 2:586, 592.
39. *Baltimore Sun,* April 22, 1861.
40. Radcliffe, *Governor Thomas H. Hicks,* 68.
41. *Official Records,* ser. 1, 2:587.
42. Ibid., ser. 1, 2:773.
43. *New York Times,* April 21, 1861.
44. Radcliffe, *Governor Thomas H. Hicks,* 66.
45. *Official Records,* ser. 1, 2:595.
46. Ibid., ser. 1, 2:596.
47. Ibid., ser. 1, 2:592.
48. *New York Times,* April 23, 1861.

49. Angle and Miers, *Tragic Years,* 83.

50. Ibid., 64–65.

51. Quoted in ibid., 83.

52. *Official Records,* ser. 1, 2:600–1.

53. Ibid.

54. *New York Times,* April 25, 1861.

55. Radcliffe, *Governor Thomas H. Hicks,* 71–73.

56. Smith, *The Borderland in the Civil War,* 6.

57. *Official Records,* ser. 1, 2:607.

58. Ibid., ser. 1, 2:603–4.

59. Ibid., ser. 1, 2:604–6.

60. Scharf, *History of Maryland,* 425–27.

61. Angle and Miers, *Tragic Years,* 67–68.

62. Festus P. Summers, *The Baltimore and Ohio in the Civil War* (1939; repr. ed., New York: Stan Clark Military Books, 1993), 58.

63. *Official Records,* ser. 1, 2:607.

64. Angle and Miers, *Tragic Years,* 67–68.

65. *Official Records,* ser. 1, 2:608–9.

66. Long, *The Civil War Day by Day,* 67.

67. Reprinted in the *Baltimore Sun,* April 30, 1861.

68. Radcliffe, *Governor Thomas H. Hicks,* 79.

69. Bradley T. Johnson, *Confederate Military History, Volume 2, Maryland* (Secarus), 30.

70. Brown, *Baltimore and the 19th of April,* 34.

71. Scharf, *History of Maryland,* 418.

72. Harold R. Manakee, *Maryland in the Civil War* (Baltimore: Maryland Historical Society, 1961), 23.

73. Wright, *The Secession Movement in the Middle-Atlantic States,* 71.

74. Brown, *Baltimore and the 19th of April,* 77.

75. Radcliffe, *Governor Thomas H. Hicks,* 79.

76. Scharf, *History of Maryland,* 424–25.

77. Crofts, *Reluctant Confederates,* 247.

Chapter 5: The End

1. Cited in Harry W. Newman, *Maryland and the Confederacy* (Annapolis: The Author, 1976), 158.

2. Clark, *Politics in Maryland during the Civil War,* 82–83.

3. Ibid., 80–81.

4. Ibid., 81–82.

5. *Official Records,* ser. 1, 2:615–16.

6. Ibid., ser. 1, 2:616.

7. *Sun,* May 1, 1861.

8. Ibid., May 2, 1861.

9. *Official Records,* ser. 1, 2:617–18.

10. *Sun,* May 7, 1861.

11. Maryland Civil War Centennial Commission, *Maryland Remembers* (Hagerstown, 1961), 5.

12. *Official Records,* ser. 1, 2:30.

13. Matthew Ellenberger, "'Whigs in the Streets'": Baltimore Republicanism in the Spring of 1861," *Maryland Historical Magazine,* 86 (1991): 32.

14. Andrews, *History of Maryland,* 521.

15. Radcliffe, *Governor Thomas H. Hicks,* 82–83.

16. Ibid., 85.

17. Scharf, *History of Maryland,* 426–27.

18. Radcliffe, *Governor Thomas H. Hicks,* 113.

19. Andrews, *History of Maryland,* 523.

20. The reader interested in further discussion should review James G. Randall, *Constitutional Problems Under Lincoln* (Urbana: University of Illinois Press, 1951).

21. Catton, *Reflections on the Civil War,* 32–33.

22. Randall and Donald, *Civil War and Reconstruction,* 304.

23. Radcliffe, *Governor Thomas H. Hicks,* 105–6.

24. *Official Records,* ser. 1, 2:104.

25. Ibid., ser. 2, 1:625.

26. Cited in Clark, *Politics in Maryland during the Civil War,* 59.

27. Scharf, *History of Maryland,* 431.

28. Manakee, *Maryland in the Civil War,* 54.

29. *Official Records,* ser. 1, 5:12.

30. Manakee, *Maryland in the Civil War,* 54–55.

31. *Official Records,* ser. 2, 1:631.

32. Ibid., ser. 2, 1:641.

33. Ibid., ser. 2, 1:589.

34. Ibid., ser. 1, 1:591–92.

35. Marks and Schatz, eds., *Between North and South,* 36.

36. *Official Records,* ser. 1, 2:760.

37. Radcliffe, *Governor Thomas H. Hicks,* 107–9.

38. *Official Records,* ser. 2, 1:678–79.

39. W. Jefferson Buchanan, *Maryland's Hope* (Richmond, 1864), 17. The secret letters from Union men of Maryland can be found in the Manuscripts Division, Maryland Historical Society, Baltimore.

40. A detailed description of the arrests can be found in the *Official Records* under the poignant heading, "The Maryland Arrests," ser. 2, 1:619–20, 667–74.

41. *Official Records,* ser. 2, 1:595.

42. Sidney T. Matthews, "Control of the Baltimore Press during the Civil War," 151.

43. Ibid.

44. Maryland Civil War Centennial Commission, *Maryland Remembers,* 7.

45. Marks and Schatz, eds., *Between North and South,* 37.

46. Charles Branch Clark and George L. P. Radcliffe, two Maryland historians, examined the election in some detail.

47. Newman, *Maryland and the Confederacy,* 60.

48. Clark, *Politics in Maryland during the Civil War,* 61, 77.

49. Ibid., 79.

50. Ibid., 81.

51. Scharf, *History of Maryland,* 459–60.

52. Radcliffe, *Governor Thomas H. Hicks,* 116–17.

53. Manakee, *Maryland in the Civil War,* 56.

54. Radcliffe, *Governor Thomas H. Hicks,* 114–18.

55. *Official Records,* ser. 1, 5:197.

56. Ibid., ser. 2, 1:705.

57. Clark, *Politics in Maryland during the Civil War,* 3, 129.

Chapter 6: The Military Issue: More Than Just Numbers

1. Catton, *Reflections on the Civil War,* 40.

2. Charles B. Clark, "Recruitment of Union Troops in Maryland, 1861–1865," *Maryland Historical Magazine,* 53 (1958): 153–54.

3. Dieter Cunz, "The Maryland Germans in the Civil War," *Maryland Historical Magazine,* 36 (1941): 305–6.

4. *Official Records,* ser. 3, 1:721.

5. Millard G. LesCallette, *A Study of the Recruitment of the Union Army in the State of Maryland, 1861–1865* (M.A. Thesis, Johns Hopkins University, 1954), 25, 37.

6. *Official Records,* ser 3, 2:206–7, 5:744–45.

7. Catton, *Reflections on the Civil War,* 56–57.

8. LesCallette, *Recruitment of the Union Army in Maryland,* 54–55.

9. Ibid., 33.

10. Ibid., 51; James M. McPherson, *Battle Cry of Freedom: The Civil War Era* (New York: Oxford University Press, 1988), 492.

11. Scharf, *History of Maryland,* 519.

12. Catton, *Reflections on the Civil War,* 57.

13. *Official Records,* ser. 3, 4:790.

14. Clark, "Recruitment of Union Troops in Maryland," 155.

15. Bradley T. Johnson, *Confederate Military History,* 98.

16. W. Darrell Overdyke, *The Know-Nothing Party in the South,* 19.

17. Cunz, "Maryland Germans in the Civil War," 394–95.

18. Ibid., 396–416.

19. Johnson, *Confederate Military History,* 98.

20. Katherine A. Harvey, "The Civil War and the Maryland Coal Trade," *Maryland Historical Magazine,* 62 (1967): 364.

21. The reader seriously interested in the numbers game should consult Daniel D. Hartzler, *Marylanders in the Confederacy* (Silver Spring, Md.: Published by the author, 1986), which chronicles nearly 10,000 Marylanders who served the South.

22. John Montgomery Gambrill, *Leading Events in Maryland History,* (Baltimore: The Cushing Co., 1903), 176.

23. Hartzler, *Marylanders in the Confederacy,* 1.

24. Johnson, *Confederate Military History,* 2:43.

25. Andrews, *History of Maryland,* 525.

26. Catton, *Reflections on the Civil War,* 230.

27. *Official Records,* ser. 3, 4:1270.

28. Clark, "Recruitment of Union Troops in Maryland," 163.

29. LesCallette, *Recruitment of the Union Army in Maryland,* 46, 69, 171–73.

Chapter 7: A Matter of Economics

1. Edward Ingle, *Southern Sidelights* (Boston, 1896), 109.

2. Herbert Wender, *Southern Commercial Conventions, 1837–1859* (Baltimore: The Johns Hopkins University Press, 1930), 20.

3. Thomas Prentice Kettell, *Southern Wealth and Northern Profits* (repr.; Montgomery: University of Alabama Press, 1965), x.

4. The reader interested in contemporary discussion on the economic issue should consult Thomas P. Kettell's *Southern Wealth and Northern Profits;* J. D. B. DeBow's *Commercial Review of the South and West;* Edward Ingle's *Southern Sidelights,* particularly the chapter "Trade and Commerce"; and Herbert Wender's *Southern Commercial Conventions, 1837–1859.*
5. Wender, *Southern Commercial Conventions,* 9.
6. Smith, *The Borderland in the Civil War,* 4.
7. Carl M. Freasure, "Union Sentiment in Maryland, 1856–60," *Maryland Historical Magazine,* 24 (1929): 214.
8. Ingle, *Southern Sidelights,* 335.
9. Crofts, *Reluctant Confederates,* 334.
10. See William B. Catton, "The Baltimore Business Community and the Secession Crisis, 1860–1861" (M.A. thesis, University of Maryland, 1952).
11. Catton, "The Baltimore Business Community," 44.
12. Ibid., 45.
13. Ibid., 47–51.
14. Ibid., 48.
15. Ibid., 54–55.
16. Ibid., 77.
17. Summers, *The Baltimore and Ohio in the Civil War,* 18.
18. Ibid., 19.
19. Ibid., 45.
20. Ibid., 46.
21. Ibid.
22. Ibid., 58–59.
23. Ibid., 213.
24. Ibid., 222–23.
25. Andrews, *History of Maryland,* 530–31.

Chapter 8: Conclusion

1. Scharf, *History of Maryland,* 294.
2. Ibid., 314.
3. Wender, *Southern Commercial Conventions,* 200.
4. Ingle, *Southern Sidelights,* 298–99.
5. Craven, *Growth of Southern Nationalism,* 400.

6. Frederick Jackson Turner, *The Significance of Sections in American History* (New York: H. Holt & Co., 1932), 337.

7. Marks and Schatz, eds., *Between North and South*, 228.

8. Allison L. Wilmer J. H. Jarrett, and George W. F. Vernon, *History and Roster of Maryland Volunteers, War of 1861–1865* (repr.; Silver Spring, Md.: Family Line Publications and Toomey Press, 1987), 1:1.

9. *Official Records*, ser. 2, 1:676.

10. Scharf, *History of Maryland*, 703.

11. John T. Willis, *Presidential Elections in Maryland* (Mt. Airy, Md.: Lomond Publications, Inc., 1984), 177.

13. Scharf, *History of Maryland*, 688.

14. Ibid., 688.

Bibliography

Anderson, Charles C. *Fighting by Southern Federals*. New York, 1912.

Andrews, Matthew Page. *History of Maryland: Province and State*. Reprint edition, Hatboro, 1965.

Angle, Paul M. and Earl Schenck Miers. *The Tragic Years 1860–1865*. 2 vols.; New York, 1960.

Ashworth, George F. "The Secession Movement in Maryland," Ph.D. diss., Georgetown University, 1934.

Baker, Jean H. *The Politics of Continuity*. Baltimore, 1973.

Baltimore Sun

Beall, George. "Persuasion of Maryland to Join the Federal Union During 1861." Senior thesis, Princeton University, 1959.

Booth, George W. *Personal Reminiscences of a Maryland Soldier in the War Between the States 1861–1865*. Reprint edition. Gaithersburg, 1986.

Brown, George W. *Baltimore and the 19th of April, 1861*. Reprint, Baltimore, 1982.

Brugger, Robert J. *Maryland, A Middle Temperment, 1634–1980*. Baltimore, 1988.

Buchanan, W. Jefferson, "Maryland's Hope." Richmond, 1864.

Carpenter, Jesse T. *The South as a Conscious Minority*. New York, 1930.

Catton, Bruce. *Reflections on the Civil War*. New York, 1982.

Catton, William B. "The Baltimore Business Community and the Secession Crisis, 1860–61." Master's Thesis, University of Maryland, 1952.

Clark, Charles B. *Politics in Maryland During the Civil War*. Chestertown, 1952.

_____. *The Eastern Shore of Maryland and Virginia*. New York, 1950.

_____. "Recruitment of Union Troops in Maryland, 1861–1865." *Maryland Historical Magazine*, 53 (1958): 153–177.

_____. "Suppression and Control of Maryland, 1861–1865." *Maryland Historical Magazine*, 54 (1959): 241–271.

Combs, James J. "The Know Nothing Party and the Unionist Movement in Maryland." B.A. Thesis, Harvard College, 1963.

Craven, Avery O. *The Growth of Southern Nationalism, 1848–1861.* New Orleans, 1953.

Crenshaw, Ollinger. *The Slave States in the Presidential Election of 1860.* Baltimore, 1945.

Crofts, Daniel W. *Reluctant Confederates.* Chapel Hill, 1989.

Cunz, Dieter. "The Maryland Germans in the Civil War." *Maryland Historical Magazine,* 36 (1941): 394–419.

Dumond, Dwight L. *The Secession Movement 1860–61.* New York, 1963.

Evitts, William J. *A Matter of Allegiances: Maryland from 1850 to 1861.* Baltimore, 1974.

Freasure, Carl M. "Union Sentiment in Maryland, 1856–60." *Maryland Historical Magazine,* 24 (1929): 210–224.

Freehling, William W. *The Reintegration of American History.* New York, 1994.

Gambrill, John M. *Leading Events in Maryland History.* Baltimore, 1903.

Gilmor, Harry. *Four Years in the Saddle.* New York, 1866.

Goldsborough, W. W. *The Maryland Line in the Confederate Army.* Reprint. Gaithersburg, 1983.

Hartzler, Daniel D. *Marylanders in the Confederacy.* Silver Spring. 1986.

Harvey, Katherine A. "The Civil War and the Maryland Coal Trade." *Maryland Historical Magazine,* 62 (1967): 361–380.

Howard, McHenry. *Recollections of a Maryland Confederate.* Baltimore, 1914.

Hurst, Harold W. "The Northernmost Southern Town: A Sketch of Pre–Civil War Annapolis." *Maryland Historical Magazine,* 76 (1981): 240–249.

Ingle, Edward. *Southern Sidelights.* Boston, 1896.

Johnson, Bradley T. *Confederate Military History.* Vol. 2. *Maryland.* Secarcus, no date.

Kettell, Thomas Prentice. *Southern Wealth and Northern Profits.* 1860. Repr., University, Alabama, 1965.

LesCallette, Millard G. "A Study of the Recruitment of the Union Army in the State of Maryland, 1861–1865." Master's Thesis, Johns Hopkins University, 1954.

Long, E. B. *The Civil War Day by Day.* New York, 1971.

Manakee, Harold R. *Maryland in the Civil War.* Baltimore, 1961.

Marks, B. E. and M. N. Schatz, eds. *Between North and South, A Maryland Journalist Views the Civil War: The Narrative of William Wilkens Glenn.* Cranbury, 1976.

Marshall, John A. *American Bastiles.* Philadelphia, 1870.

Maryland Civil War Centennial Commission. *Maryland Remembers.* Hagerstown, 1961.

Matthews, Sidney T. "Control of the Baltimore Press during the Civil War." *Maryland Historical Magazine,* 36 (1941): 150–170.

McKim, Randolph H. *A Soldier's Recollections.* New York, 1910.

Meyers, William Starr. "Governor Bradford's Private List of Union Men in 1861." *Maryland Historical Magazine,* 7 (1912): 83–90.

_____. *The Self-Reconstruction of Maryland, 1864–1867.* Johns Hopkins University Studies in Historical and Political Science, vol. 27. Baltimore, 1909.

New York Times

Newman, Harry W. *Maryland and the Confederacy.* Annapolis, 1 976.

Nicholson, Issac F. "The Maryland Guard Battalion, 1860–61." *Maryland Historical Magazine,* 6 (1911): 117–131.

Nicolay, John G. and John Hay. *Abraham Lincoln: A History.* New York, 1890.

Overdyke, W. Darrell. *The Know-Nothing Party in the South.* Binghamton, 1950.

Radcliffe, George L. P. *Governor Thomas H. Hicks of Maryland and the Civil War.* Johns Hopkins University Studies in Historical and Political Science, Vol. 19. Baltimore, 1901.

Randall, James G. *Constitutional Problems under Lincoln.* Urbana, 1951.

Randall, J. G. and David Donald. *The Civil War and Reconstruction.* Boston, 1961.

Rawley, James A. *Turning Points of the Civil War.* Lincoln, 1989.

Scharf, J. Thomas. *History of Maryland.* Reprint. Hatboro, 1967.

Schlesinger, A. M. and Fred L. Israel. *History of American Presidential Elections 1789–1968.* New York, 1971.

Seabrook, William L. W. "Maryland's Great Part in Saving the Union." Pamphlet by Author, 1913.

"Secret Letters from Union Men in Maryland." Maryland Historical Society Library, Rare Book Section.

Shanks, Henry T. *The Secession Movement in Virginia 1847–1861.* Richmond, 1934.

Simkins, Francis Butler. *A History of the South.* New York, 1953.

Smith, Edward C. *The Borderland in the Civil War.* Freeport, 1927

Summers, Festus P. *The Baltimore and Ohio in the Civil War.* New York, 1939.

Tatum, Georgia Lee. *Disloyalty in the Confederacy.* Chapel Hill, 1934.

Thomas, David Y. "Southern Non-Slaveholders in the Election of 1860." *Political Science Quarterly,* 26 (1911): 222–34.

Toomey, Daniel C. *The Civil War in Maryland.* Baltimore, 1983.

Turner, Frederick Jackson. *The Significance of Sections in American History.* New York, 1932.

Walmsley, James E. "The Change of Secession Sentiment in Virginia in 1861." *American Historical Review,* 31 (1925): 180–219.

Walsh, Richard and William Lloyd Fox, eds. *Maryland: A History, 1632–1974.* Baltimore, 1974.

War of the Rebellion, Official Records of the Union and Confederate Armies. Washington, 1881–1900.

Wender, Herbert. *Southern Commercial Conventions, 1837–1859.* Baltimore, 1930.

Willis, John T. *Presidential Elections in Maryland.* Mt. Airy, 1984.

Wilmer, L. Allison, J. H. Jarrett, and Geo. W. F. Vernon. *History and Roster of Maryland Volunteers, War of 1861–1865.* Vol. 1. Reprint. Silver Spring, 1987.

Wright, William C. *The Secession Movement in the Middle Atlantic States.* Rutherford, 1973.

INDEX